DATE YOUR WORTH, NOT
YOUR WOUND

RACHEL ROSE

DATE YOUR WORTH, NOT YOUR WOUND

DISCLAIMER:
The information in this book is based on the author's personal and professional experience and is intended for educational and inspirational purposes only. It is not a substitute for professional, medical, psychological, financial, or legal advice. Readers are encouraged to use their own judgment and seek qualified support where appropriate. The author and publisher disclaim any responsibility or liability for any loss, damage, or outcomes resulting from the use of this material. By reading this book, you acknowledge responsibility for your own choices, well-being, and results. Individual experiences will vary, and specific outcomes are not guaranteed, as success in love and growth depends on each reader's unique circumstances. For privacy and confidentiality, all client names and identifying details have been changed, and some composite examples are used. Any resemblance to real persons, living or dead, is purely coincidental.

Tradepaper ISBN: 978-1-0369-1628-2
E-book ISBN: 978-1-0369-3486-6

Copyright © 2025 by Rachel Rose Online
All rights reserved. No part of this book may be reproduced in any manner whatsoever without written permission from the author except in the case of brief quotations embodied in critical articles and reviews.

First Printing, 2025

Cover design by Ekaterina Sidorenko

Copy editing by Susan Keillor

Author photograph © Rachel Rose Online
All rights reserved. No part of this image may be reproduced, stored, or transmitted in any form or by any means, electronic or mechanical, including photocopying, recording, or any information storage or retrieval system, without prior written permission from the author.

A Note on Inclusivity

This book, along with the author's other works and marketing materials, focuses on heterosexual women in relationships with men, reflecting her personal experience and her clients' experience, though the principles may be applied to other dynamics if they resonate. The language and examples used are not intended to exclude or discriminate against any gender identity or sexual orientation, and the intention of this work is to support all readers in creating healthier, more self-aware, and fulfilling relationships regardless of how they identify or who they love.

I dedicate this book to all the different versions of myself it took to get here. To the strength it took to survive, to heal, and to choose differently not just for me, but for the generations of women who will follow.

CONTENTS

Dedication
vi

— Introduction
1

— PART ONE: Awareness
7

1 — The High Achiever's Dilemma in Love
9

2 — Dating Your Worth: The Foundation
15

— PART TWO: Healing
31

3 — Healing Your Wounds: The Inner Work
33

4 — The Three Core Love Wounds: Abandonment Wound
46

5 — The Three Core Love Wounds: Unworthiness Wound
52

6 — The Three Core Love Wounds: Control Wound
61

7 — Trust: The Foundation of Lasting Love
66

— PART THREE: Embodiment
78

8 — Redefining Love for the Modern Woman
80

9 — The Standards Reset
89

10 — Feminine Energy Meets Ambition
101

11 — Mastering the Dating Funnel
112

12 — Attracting Your Equal
121

13 — The Art of Commitment
133

— PART FOUR: Expansion
144

14 — The Abundant You: Love and Wealth in Alignment
146

15 — Living Your Highest Love Timeline
153

— Conclusion: You Are Worthy of it All
164

– The Love and Alignment Toolkit
168

– Recommended Reading
177

– Epilogue: The Evolution of You
179

– Acknowledgements
183

About the Author
186

INTRODUCTION

THE MYTH OF CHOOSING BETWEEN LOVE AND SUCCESS

Have you ever told yourself, "I'm too busy to date?" Or maybe you've convinced yourself that love will just "happen" someday, once your calendar finally clears or you've hit that next big milestone in your career.

You're not alone. For many high-achieving women, dating often feels like a luxury, rather than a necessity. It almost feels like it has turned into something to squeeze into the gaps between meetings, presentations and all the other demands of a successful life. But let's be honest: Is it really about being too busy? Or is "too busy" a shield you use to protect yourself from the vulnerability that comes with putting yourself out there?

For years, I used the "too busy" excuse myself. I poured my energy into my career, and every promotion. Every accolade or achievement felt like proof that I was doing the right thing. I was climbing the ladder, breaking barriers and making a name for myself in my field. My life looked perfect from the outside...impressive even. But behind the scenes, I was lonely, overworked and deeply unfulfilled.

I had convinced myself that love could wait. That I would focus on finding a relationship once everything else was in order. But that day never came. Work always had another demand. My goals were a moving target. And as I continued to "wait for the right time," I watched years go by without building the kind of meaningful relationship I craved. I told myself, "If it's meant to happen, it will." I said things like, "If he wanted to, he would," thinking that was some kind of mantra for empowerment. But the truth? I wasn't showing up for love at all. I was waiting for something magical to happen, *when I wasn't doing anything to create the conditions for it.*

One day, I had a realization that shook me to my core: The corporation I was working so hard for would continue to thrive without me. It would keep making millions long after I burned out. I realized I could give it my all for decades and still be left wondering what I was really working for. That wake-up call forced me to face the truth. The problem wasn't my schedule. The problem was the stories I told myself about love, success, and my own worth. And if you're holding this book, chances are you might have told yourself those same stories, too.

This book is for women like you: high-achieving leaders and visionaries who know they're capable of extraordinary things but still feel like love is out of reach. You've probably asked yourself questions like:

"Why does dating feel so much harder for me than it does for other people?"

"Why do I keep attracting men who don't match my energy, my ambition, or my values?"

"Is it even possible to have the kind of love I want without sacrificing the success I've worked so hard to achieve?"

I'm here to tell you that it absolutely is possible. You don't have to choose between love and success. You don't have to settle for mediocrity in your personal life just because you refuse to settle in your professional one. You don't have to wait for the stars to align before you can experience the partnership you desire. You just need the tools to step into your worth, heal the wounds that keep you stuck, and start showing up for love with the same intention and purpose you bring to every other area of your life. Above all, having the willingness to not only do love differently, but to also experience it differently is what matters most of all.

WHY "TOO BUSY" ISN'T THE PROBLEM

Let's go back to the phrase, "I'm too busy to date." It's something we've all said at one point or another, but what does it really mean? On the surface, it feels logical. Your days are packed with 101+ responsibilities. By the time you get home, you're too drained to even think about swiping on dating apps, let alone going out and meeting someone. The hard truth about that though is this: the "too busy" excuse is often a cover for deeper fears and limiting beliefs about love.

For many high-achieving women, "too busy" actually means:

"I'm afraid of being vulnerable."

"I don't believe I'm worthy of the kind of love I really want."

"I don't want to fail in my personal life because of the way that I've succeeded in my career."

"I'm scared that if I prioritize love, I'll lose the momentum I've worked so hard to build."

Sound familiar? These beliefs don't make you weak or flawed; they make you human. However, unless you address them head-on, they'll continue to block you from experiencing the love you deserve. When I look back on my own journey, I can see now that I wasn't really too busy to date. *I was hiding.* I was scared of rejection, afraid of losing my independence, and unsure how to even begin navigating a dating world that felt completely foreign to me. I know how tempting it is to stay in that safe, comfortable place where "work comes first." But I also know how unfulfilling that place can be if that is *all you have*.

RECLAIMING SPACE FOR LOVE

The truth is, love doesn't require you to sacrifice your ambition. It doesn't ask you to choose between success and partnership. But it *does* ask you to be intentional. If you want to create space for love in your life, you need to start treating it like the priority it deserves to be. That means letting go of the "too busy" excuse and making an active decision to show up for love...even when it feels uncomfortable or inconvenient. This doesn't mean you have to upend your entire life or put your career on hold. It means learning how to integrate dating into your life in a way that feels aligned, sustainable and, above all, empowering.

And that's exactly what this book is here to help you do.

WHAT YOU'LL DISCOVER IN THIS BOOK

In the chapters ahead, we'll explore how to:

- **Heal the wounds that keep you stuck in unhealthy patterns:** whether it's childhood programming, past heartbreak, or societal expectations, we'll uncover the root causes of self-sabotage, so that you can start building the foundation for healthy, fulfilling relationships.

- **Date your worth, not your wound:** you'll learn how to stop settling for less and start attracting partners who are truly aligned with your values, vision, and of course, your worth.

- **Balance love and ambition:** we'll bust the myth that dating has to feel like a full-time job and explore practical strategies for integrating love into your busy life.

- **Show up with confidence and clarity:** from setting boundaries to communicating your needs, you'll develop the tools to navigate the dating world with intention and self-assurance.

This isn't just a book about dating. It's a guide to reclaiming your belief in love and your power to create the life and relationship you want.

Let's Begin

This book is your invitation to rewrite the story you've been telling yourself about love. It's a roadmap to finding the partnership you deserve but without sacrificing the ambition and independence that make you who you are.

In fact, this book is for those of you who know that if push comes to shove, you could be in a relationship with *any* man tomorrow. But you're here reading this book because you are part of what I like to call, the top 1% of the world. And no, I am not just referring to your income; your value is so much more than what is in your bank account. I am talking about your ability to establish yourself as a powerhouse in a world that wasn't necessarily built for you. You're the kind of woman who people can easily identify as being the trailblazer in the family. You may be a generational cycle breaker at that too. You know you're different. You know you have something special to offer. And therefore, you don't need a book to just tell you how to get a boyfriend for the season. What you deeply desire is a Goliath of a partner who you can take over the world with and build an empire with. And that takes a completely different strategy than just showing up and hoping love will just fall in your lap.

So, if you're truly ready to do this entire love thing differently, congratulations! You are in exactly the right place. I also warn you that I am a proud Virgo sun woman with an Aries moon, a Gemini ascendant and a Venus in Scorpio placement. Translation? I don't do ordinary, and therefore, if you're entering my coaching world, know that my motto is **high risk, high reward**. That's to say, the work I gift you will challenge the hell out of you and force you to get comfortable with being uncomfortable. This is all in exchange for you attracting the biggest and deepest soulmate connections that you have yet to experience.

PART ONE: AWARENESS

"The moment you realize that achievement isn't the enemy at all and that avoidance is...everything shifts". — *Rachel Rose*

CHAPTER 1

THE HIGH ACHIEVER'S DILEMMA IN LOVE

Let's start with the obvious: Ambition is not the problem. Your drive, your passion, your independence...none of these are *liabilities*. **They are gifts.** They make you magnetic and powerful. But when unbalanced, ambition can quietly bleed into your personal life in ways that create disconnection and misalignment.

The mindset that fuels your career often centers around control, problem-solving, and achievement. In relationships, however, healthy and sustainable love doesn't thrive under control. It thrives under vulnerability, trust, and mutual effort. Read that again. *Let it truly land for you for a moment.*

Many high-achieving women subconsciously apply their "CEO mindset" to their dating lives in a way that is unknowingly destructive. For example, you may find yourself:

- Taking the lead in conversations, planning dates (even subtly), and following up whenever there is a drop in pace and continuity.

- Treating the men you date as a project by trying to "fix" or "help" them in ways they should be doing for themselves.

- Over-giving emotionally, energetically, and/or financially and, as a result, tipping the scales over entirely and creating an imbalance.

- Dismissing men who don't meet arbitrary success metrics (such as not having bought their first home by 30 or leasing their car and not owning it outright), even if they offer the level of emotional richness that you know would complement your soul beautifully.

- Prioritizing your career so much that you leave little room for emotional intimacy, because you are, in fact, already dating your business and/or your corporate job.

Dating therefore feels like another task on your to-do list rather than an enriching, enjoyable experience. *And that is the reason why you're so resentful of it.*

THE INDEPENDENCE TRAP

Another common challenge is what I call "The Independence Trap." Society has celebrated the image of the strong, independent woman who doesn't need anyone. And while independence is powerful, when weaponized, it becomes a wall rather than a boundary.

You might find yourself thinking that you don't need a man and that you can do it all by yourself. Perhaps you even think that there is no man on the planet who isn't taken already who will ever meet your level of success. But that level of independence can quietly become a form of self-protection, convincing you that needing no one keeps you safe when in reality it keeps love out.

This way of thinking is exactly what my client, who we will call, Amelia, used to do. I met her, and she *thought* she was ready for love. We discussed everything she felt that made her ready for a serious partnership and yes, it made sense why she was now wondering what was taking the Universe so long to deliver her the goods. She truly was a one in a million type of woman with her life together and a magnetic aura you could not put a price on if you tried. She lit up the room, for sure. But what was so interesting and something that I pointed out to her is that her regular day-to-day energy said feminine AF, but when it came to men, it was like there was a dark cloud hovering above her. I knew she wanted to call in her soulmate, but she was not ready to put down the impenetrable armor she had put up that she believed was keeping her protected from unsafe men. And it was...but it was also keeping her lonely and away from all the ones who could meet her where she was at.

We discussed all of her mantras that kept her glued in this mindset, not to mention the fact she had so many of them plastered all over her house to reinforce her programming. Now, even though this is such a great way of helping you to build new neural pathways, in this situation, the wrong mantras can also isolate you from connection. It wasn't long before working with her, a matter of weeks in fact, that by putting this armor down she was able to manifest her very own soulmate...ironically this man had been orbiting her the whole time and was waiting for the moment to get in touch! Talk about the Universe doing what it does best, and never allowing anything to miss you that is meant for you!

The point I am trying to make here is that love is not a business transaction. It requires openness, receptivity, and trust. These qualities are often left untapped when you're stuck in achievement mode. As a result, you are sending off signals to the world that your cup is all the way full for yourself and that is enough. Since God, Spirit, the angels, and the Universe cannot override your free will, this is why you are still in this cycle. The good thing is this is a train that has multiple stops and you are being encouraged to get off as soon as you can, as "the longer you stay on the wrong train, the harder it is to get home" — or so the saying goes.

Why Success in Your Career Doesn't Always Translate to Love

The truth is, the systems that reward you in your career are fundamentally different from the dynamics that nourish romantic relationships.

In your career: The more you control, the more you achieve.

In love: The more you surrender, the more you receive.

This isn't to say that you should shrink yourself or play small. *Definitely none of that, please, around here!* It's about recognizing that love requires a different skill-set, and that is one rooted in emotional availability. It requires being seen for who you *really* are. The question is — and this can also be a journal prompt for yourself — *who are you without your titles?* As in *you* at your core? Many high-achieving women struggle with this question because they view themselves, and even approach dating, through a professional lens. They lead with their career identity, not their emotional truth. The problem with this is that love isn't a project to be managed or a goal to be achieved; it's an experience to be felt and co-created with another person.

Common Pitfalls for High-Achieving Women in Love

If you recognize yourself in Amelia's story, you're not alone. Hyper-independence isn't a trait that any of us are born with but rather, it is learned through early childhood conditioning as a survival tactic. By refusing to lean on anyone emotionally or physically, this is a direct manifestation of the experiences you had growing up that taught you that you must do it all on your own, because nobody else was going to do it for you. This can result in emotional guarding in many different forms. For instance, this can include keeping conversations surface-level and avoiding vulnerability for fear of appearing "needy"; blocking and deleting romantic prospects over the smallest thing that you dislike and never really taking any accountability of the part you play in repeated relationship dynamics that become patterns.

Hyper-independence also manifests as perfectionism. This can be seen in the way that you apply the same high-pressure standards to love as you do in your career, which can make dating feel exhausting and unfulfilling. I love that women in our day and age have beautifully high standards, but the key here is to remember that we are all human. Sadly, even though social media has its obvious benefits, it feels like it has skewed a lot of our way of screening potential matches. We are flooded with beautiful men all the time from around the world with their perfectly sculpted bodies, five-star getaways, and carefully crafted versions of success. Somewhere along the line, that became the standard of what makes a man desirable. Do not forget that social media and, as a result, sometimes dating app profiles, are a highlight reel — you need to genuinely get to know someone's soul before writing them off. Or...end up as one of those women who are basically married to their careers and look back in a decade or two and wonder how much of their lives they didn't get to spend with someone special.

CHAPTER 2

DATING YOUR WORTH: THE FOUNDATION

You've scaled mountains in your professional life and shattered glass ceilings. Despite this being the case, when it comes to dating, you're feeling stuck, tired, and maybe you are endlessly circling the "talking stage" without anything real coming out of it. Why? Because the very skills that made you successful in business can often keep you in patterns of over-giving and settling for less in relationships.

This chapter is about outlining how to step into your full worth as a high-value woman in dating. Ironically though, even though you are wired to be hardworking and go all in when it comes to anything you want, it is likely that you have fallen into a common trap. That trap is thinking that dating is just something that will just fall into your lap eventually without any real strategy. It's a strange paradox because your natural instinct is to plan, organize, and make things happen, yet part of you still hopes your love life will just *magically* work out. But if that mindset had worked, you wouldn't be holding this book right now.

This book is not just about having a partner. For someone like you, that's fairly easy. In fact, the truth is when people ask you that dreaded question, "Why are you single?", or even worse, "Why have you been single for *so long*?"...there is a part of you that just quietly lets this person get away with their judgment. This is because deep down, you know that you *could* have just anyone...if you truly wanted to. You have had, and still probably have as you read this book, multiple men who would happily get into a committed relationship with you tomorrow and ride off into the sunset.

When you look at some of the people you know, for some of these women, you can definitely see why they are with their partners and why they are a match. You can see them and think, "Wow, that is an inspiration."

And then there are other women that may even be very close to you or even related to you, and you just know, having known them for a significant period of their lives, that they have settled...*big time*. You know what they *actually* wanted, and from what they have told you about their partner, this person doesn't really check a lot of their boxes.

So why did they choose people who fell short of their deepest desires? I personally believe that everyone has their reasons for this, but regardless of how many different ways a woman can explain it — it usually comes down to this one thing. Pressure. Societal pressure. And it is usually wrapped around time, either because a woman's biological clock is ticking or that her perceived shelf life is expiring. In other words, the message is: *just pick anybody before you're left with nobody.*

I know that the thought has crossed your mind maybe once or twice. I know because I have been there. I have been exactly where you are, and instead of just settling because it was marriage o'clock, I decided to bet on myself instead of just caving into "good enough." "Good enough" is only good enough if you are comfortable with never being in a relationship where you are truly inspired to step into the best version of yourself. If you're comfortable not feeling like you are with someone with a purpose as strong as yours. If you're comfortable being with someone who you do not share any passions with. If you're comfortable being with someone who is happy to drain you of all your energy, whilst you endlessly pour yourself into them. And of course, that is not the life you envisioned for yourself and your future other half.

Dating your worth on the other hand, means you're no longer chasing or staying stuck in emotionally burdensome situations. It's about reclaiming your time, energy, and standards, and it starts with understanding the difference between dating your wounds and dating your worth.

This chapter is for laying down the foundation to help you transform your dating life by putting your worth front and center, once and for all.

DATING YOUR WOUNDS VS. DATING YOUR WORTH

What does this actually mean? Have you ever dated someone who mirrored your insecurities instead of your greatness? Maybe you found yourself excusing bad behavior, settling for bare-minimum effort, or waiting on someone to "get it together." These patterns often stem from unhealed wounds. But let's get one thing straight: **You don't date to heal your wounds. You heal your wounds so you can date your worth.**

One of the key reasons why you may have found dating almost like an uphill battle is that you have had things in reverse this entire time. That isn't to say that you can only show up to date when you are "fully healed" — the truth of the matter is that there is no such thing as being fully ready. There is such a thing, however, as running before you can walk. Your past doesn't need to be perfect for you to find love. Even if your life hasn't been linear or your parents didn't model the kind of love you desire, you are still fully capable of dating and creating a healthy relationship. What is required is that you show up authentically in your dating experience as the person who has taken accountability for their own baggage, instead of allowing the emotional residue from this to spill over into every romantic interaction.

What Does It Mean to Date Your Wounds?

Dating your wounds looks like:

Attracting Emotionally Unavailable Partners

I want to say once and for all — you are not cursed. And no, the reason why you find it tricky to find a partner is not because you simply can't "do love." These are some of the very common conclusions that women lean towards when I ask them why they feel like they haven't manifested the type of success in romantic relationships that they desire. The truth is that every partner that you come across is a mirror for what is going on internally for you.

I have had periods in my life that I like to call "transition modes." In transition mode, it is extremely difficult to attract the highest quality man because as a high-achieving woman, you are not anchored in satisfaction with your current reality. As a result, you tend to magnetize lower quality partners because, deep down, you have a fear of being truly seen. This fear comes from you treating your life like a masterpiece in progress (as you should!), but because you are *so* into the details and have your worth tied so closely to your achievements, you have the childlike way of dealing with love in which you don't want anyone to see the unfinished version of you before it's complete.

There is a hidden shame that lingers in transition mode. It is a sense that because you're not fully where you want to be, you're somehow not enough. This fear of being seen as "half-finished", in turn, creates a wall that prevents you from truly opening up to your partner. For this reason, this energy often draws in partners who are emotionally unavailable and/or in their own version of transition. As a result, they will often mirror your guardedness, and this can equate to two people unable to fully show up for each other, robbing you both of a chance of a healthy and fulfilling relationship.

But what about the women who aren't in transition mode, have a good degree of stability in other areas of their lives and still attract emotionally unavailable men? In these situations, there's often a degree of unavailability within themselves that stems from unresolved past issues. These can take many forms, but they all trace back to one core truth: They believe they want real commitment and intimacy, yet on a soul level, they're not fully ready to receive it. As a result, they can also attract someone who mirrors that same emotional limitation, like a magnet.

This dynamic can drive you crazy if you're not conscious of your own patterning. It can make you believe that all men are emotionally unavailable or "not ready for anything real," when in truth, you're unconsciously mirroring that very energy, and therefore not reflecting safety or emotional openness back to them either.

Prioritizing Potential Over Reality

Potential feels so exciting because essentially it's not real. I like to say that potential is about 20% of the reality you are dealing with when dating someone new. This means that for a very active imagination, prioritizing potential allows your brain to sometimes manufacture someone's personality to be in alignment with who you want them to be, rather than who they actually are. The benefit? If someone's potential can be inflated in your mind, this creates an illusion of control.

Theoretically, leaning more towards a new person's potential can allow you to believe that they can never fail you, because there is always the safety that "the best is yet to be realized." This is the abandoned child fallacy, in which you believe that if you just hold the high vibe and stay hopeful, the love you give to another person will inspire them to change into someone who meets all of your emotional needs, the way someone significant in your childhood failed to.

On a date, one thing I harp on so much about to my clients is that they regularly take the time to ground themselves, if necessary, multiple times during a date (and I show the different ways to do this in private coaching). A quick and easy way that you can do this is to just use your bathroom breaks to take big inhales and exhales to recenter yourself.

This is a way for you to recollect your energy and bring yourself back to the present moment, without getting too swept up in the excitement of possibility i.e. no, you are not two years deep into a relationship with this person choosing decorations for your destination wedding. You just met them. And you are effectively still dealing with someone you barely know.

Over-Explaining Your Value

One of the worst feelings in the world is that awful pit in your stomach when it is clear that the power scales have tipped, and you subconsciously can tell that you are now giving more than you're receiving. It's such a rubbish feeling. And depending on how comfortable you are with this, you may feel one of two things. Either that there is nothing you can do about it and do nothing, or you jump into chaser mode and start doing all sorts of somersaults to get this person's attention. This could be through social media, actual direct contact with them, or by resorting to protest behavior (e.g. sending them lengthy and emotionally charged messages, performing dramatic exits by blocking them on all platforms, calling their phone incessantly etc.). This is all in an attempt to try and get this person to actually *see* you. Again, this is another childhood fallacy of *"If I can just do enough, then they will see me and see my value."*

This scenario can become particularly complicated when you are dating someone who knows exactly how to push your buttons. Even more so if they act from their own unhealed wound and benefit from the continued attention you give them. Deep down, they may know they don't deserve it. They still may, however, encourage it — especially because the more your effort escalates, the more this heightens their own sense of validation.

Over-Staying in Situationships

This one is extremely common, and I am sure you have been in at least ONE situationship in your life. We are talking about the kind of relationships that never seem to get to the commitment stage. No matter how good the last time you spent was, no matter how many friends or relatives you introduce this person to or talk to about — it just *never* seems to get over the line! It just remains in this nothing-ship. Wedding invitations come and go and maybe you have even taken them as your plus one. But you are always riddled with that dreaded feeling of wondering if someone is going to ask you if your casual buddy is your partner, without you ever having had the conversation to truly define the relationship.

The painful thing about situationships is this — no matter how great the connection is, whether it be physical, emotional, sexual, spiritual or all of the above...*it is virtually impossible for this type of dynamic to survive long term.* This is not just because human relationships naturally need to develop and have milestones to mark progression, but it is also because a situationship is never a sign of TWO healthy individuals. It is usually a sign that there is at least one person with an avoidant attachment style. The other person is either also avoidant, anxiously attached, or a rare mixture of both (don't worry, we'll dive deeper into attachment styles in the next chapter). Notice how I didn't mention either of the people involved being securely attached? **That is because where** there is secure attachment, a fear of commitment cannot coexist. A securely attached person in a situationship position would at some point either obtain the next level of commitment with their partner, or they would have walked away as soon as it was apparent that progressing the relationship was not an option.

Now, are there anomalies to this? Of course, there are! But when you hear about anyone developing anything real and labeled from a situationship, just know that they had adjacent spiritual awakenings with their partner, and that does not happen every day. You are far too precious to bet your worth on a small chance, when there are plenty of high-value men who would walk over hot coals to be with you. We are here on Earth in this lifetime for a finite period, so do not sell yourself short for a lottery-win chance at love when it can be so much easier and available to you in other ways.

What Does It Mean to Date Your Worth?

Dating your worth looks a lot different from this. Some of what I am about to mention may be completely obvious to you. Some things you may be partially doing or have done in the past, and some of what I mention will sound like a foreign language.

In a nutshell, dating your worth is centered around only entertaining people who match what you're bringing to the table. It means confidently and unapologetically moving on from anyone who cannot meet your standards, without fear of loss. There is little to no second guessing your dating choices, because you have the unshakable trust that you are worth so much more than anyone who is non-committal could ever give you.

It involves mastering the art of seeing rejection as redirection; divine protection against what was never going to be the best dynamic for you and your greatness for the long term. Dating your worth means getting on board with the unpopular belief, which is: **there is no such thing as a failed relationship — every single one of them are gifts that help shape you into the next version of yourself.**

And finally, dating your worth is about these three words: quality over quantity. It's a realization that all you want to do is be in one ideal, solid, and healthy relationship at a time. There is ONE vacancy open, and a really specialist skill-set is required. You therefore don't need 50 candidates a month that vaguely fit the bill, *if at all.* Your next soulmate relationship could be just a date away, and it is walking into interactions with that vibration that is going to set you apart from those who are in the dating game thinking it is already rigged against them.

The choice to date your worth requires a mindset shift. It's a commitment to yourself, your boundaries, and your very own, tailored vision for love. It means having the guts to deconstruct any idea of love that anyone has projected onto you, and that you have taken on as your own reality. It means daring to do things differently. It means being bold enough to stand up for love in a room full of people who would rather complain about it, than take back their power and morph their own experience into something that empowers them.

TO SUMMARIZE...

Dating Your Wound looks like staying in conversations with men who show little effort, or simplifying your dating profile to not sound like you want something "too serious" because you don't want to scare any of them off.

It's over-investing your energy, hoping that your persistence will make someone choose you as a way to soothe and heal your core wound(s). It's ignoring red flags because deep down you're afraid of being alone and have latched onto the belief that there are only a handful of decent men left on the planet.

Dating Your Worth, on the other hand, is an entirely different energy. It's choosing to walk away from anyone who doesn't match your standards, not because you're bitter, but because you know you deserve better.

It's showing up in your full authenticity, trusting that the right man will see and appreciate your value without you having to convince him. It's consistently remembering why you are in the dating game in the first place...you are not dating aimlessly.

There is a very fixed goal you are trying to achieve, and in the process? There will be many prospects that will engage in the auditioning process, but only ONE gets to make it to the final round. The conditions for them to win are not impossible, but they are challenging on purpose. This is so that you are only uniting in a soulmate relationship with someone who truly is a mirror of who you are.

BONUS TRAINING

THE SCIENCE OF ATTRACTION: HOW HIGH-ACHIEVING WOMEN CAN REWIRE FOR REAL EMOTIONAL INTIMACY

If you're reading this and feeling like I just described your dating life, you're not alone. Women everywhere like yourself struggle with these patterns, not because they aren't worthy of love, but because no one ever taught them how to date in alignment with their worth. That's why I created the training, *The Science of Attraction: How High-Achieving Women Can Rewire for Real Emotional Intimacy* .

In this training, I help you understand the psychology and energetics of attraction so you can create deep emotional connection without dimming your ambition or authenticity. You will discover:

1. Why your success-driven wiring can sometimes interfere with emotional connection.

2. How to realign your success without sacrificing your ambition.

3. How attraction isn't just chemistry, it's energy and perception.

4. How high-achieving women can unintentionally project self-sufficiency in ways that block deeper intimacy.

This training is about understanding that true magnetism isn't about doing more. It's about being seen in your power from a place of ease and emotional intelligence. When you reset your approach in dating, everything changes. You're no longer chasing love; you're attracting it, all whilst remaining the accomplished woman you worked so hard to become.

HOW TO ACCESS YOUR BONUS TRAINING

1. **Go to** https://www.rachelroseonline.com/ .

2. **Select "Video Trainings."**

3. **Select the relevant training for this chapter and use code "YOUAREWORTHY" at checkout for free access.**

PART ONE: JOURNAL REFLECTIONS AND AFFIRMATIONS

Awareness is where every transformation begins. It's the moment you stop repeating your old story long enough to realize...*you wrote it*. For high-achieving women, this awareness is everything because you've built your success through logic, planning, and control. But love doesn't follow formulas.

This section invites you to notice where your patterns, fears, and beliefs might be guiding your heart more than your true self.

PROMPTS:

1. **Patterns That Repeat**
   Think about your last few romantic experiences. What's the common thread? Is it emotional unavailability, inconsistency, or over-functioning on your part?
   What patterns do I see repeating, and what might they be trying to teach me?

2. **Emotional Triggers**
   When something bothers you in dating, it's not random — it's data.
   What situations or emotions tend to trigger me most, and what deeper needs might they be revealing?

3. **Defining Safety**

   Love can't flourish without safety because both are emotional and energetic.

   What does safety in love mean to me, and how do I currently create or block it?

4. **Achievement as Protection**

   Many women use work as armor.

   In what ways do I use my ambition, independence, or success to protect myself from vulnerability?

5. **Authenticity in Love**

   Imagine you no longer had to prove or perform.

   If I could date and love freely, without fear or pretense, who would I be?

PART TWO: HEALING

―――――――――

"When you finally learn that you must integrate your pain rather than run from it, this is when you are able to love without fear". — *Rachel Rose*

CHAPTER 3

HEALING YOUR WOUNDS: THE INNER WORK

When it comes to love, we often focus on the external. For example, how to meet the right person, how to navigate dating apps, or even how to communicate effectively. The real work, however, begins within.

Believe me when I say that I have had countless women tell me that as a result of the way they grew up, their age, their race, etc., that this is the reason why they are not where they want to be when it comes to love. And with so much respect, I reply that this is BS. Why? Because when it comes to literally anything in life, there are always multiple realities available for you to buy into.

In this instance, yes, there are plenty of women who are single and have been for many years. For some of them, they seem to only be able to attract emotionally unavailable men, no matter how hard they try or how many places they move to. This isn't because they are completely out of luck, and neither are you if you're resonating with this. Our inner wounds are like tattoos — no matter where we go, they are always going to be with us. And just like with actual tattoos — you have a choice, as with all things.

Choice Number One: You can pretend they're not there. The consequence of this is that, by doing so, you may convince yourself and maybe even fool a couple of people temporarily. But the fact of the matter is they are still visible and evident for everyone to see.

Choice Number Two: You confront the skeletons in your closet and give yourself a chance to truly experience love the way it was designed to be: expansive, freeing and devastatingly beautiful — *flaws and all.*

Healing your emotional wounds is not just about addressing the past; it's about setting the foundation for the future. Until you've done the inner work, the right partner can stand in front of you, and you might not even recognize him. Worse, you may unconsciously push him away.

In the following chapters, we'll look at:

- Understanding your emotional wounds (including the core love wounds that block real intimacy).

- How unhealed wounds manifest as self-sabotage.

- Why healing is foundational to attracting the relationship you deserve.

- Attachment styles and how your wounds affect how you bond with others.

- The art of rebuilding self-trust.

- Actionable steps to begin your healing journey.

UNDERSTANDING YOUR EMOTIONAL WOUNDS

Emotional wounds are the invisible scars left behind by past experiences. Whether it's a heartbreak or childhood trauma, these wounds shape how you see yourself and others in relationships. They whisper lies like, "You're not enough," or "love always ends in betrayal."

While you might think you've moved on, these unhealed wounds often manifest in subtle yet destructive ways. You may find yourself being drawn to people who mirror the emotional unavailability of a parent or past partner. **It feels familiar even when it doesn't feel good.** This is what can confuse you and also the people around you. You may have an experience where you put up with so much and you have had close people around you question how you, a highly intuitive and intelligent woman, would ever tolerate so much confusion and mistreatment.

The truth is, our brain is a beautiful creation that prioritizes keeping you safe. Safety, however, doesn't always mean something that is good for you; it can mean something that isn't unknown.

When you are operating in this way after having had a continuous experience of men who treat you badly or give you the bare minimum, it strengthens a neural pathway that sends the message that this is your normal, and that is what is to be expected. If this becomes what is familiar to you, *anything* outside of this treatment can be deemed as "unsafe." This will remain your normal standard without real, intentional re-programming that is sparked from your own willingness to experience something different in your romantic life.

This is why it is so common that when a woman has either never had a healthy relationship or has very scarce experience in one, when a genuine person enters their life, they immediately are suspicious. Something as normal as reciprocity, emotional availability and consistency can become warning signs because you have interpreted this behavior as being too good to be true.

When fear kicks in, it can be a slippery slope, and you can subconsciously sabotage what is genuinely a great connection all because you feel it is alien to you and therefore, a threat to your peace. I want you to know that there is absolutely nothing wrong with you, as I know from my own experience, every now and then that thought can pop up when you do meet someone who appears to be a nice guy. It's totally fine and fixable, and this is why you're here with me in the trenches of this book to figure out how to turn these habits around.

What can also happen though is that you could also be a woman who swings the other way, and finds herself over-giving and over-proving a lot in the early stages of getting to know someone. This can come from a place of feeling like if you gave the relationship all of your attention and controlled the dynamics a bit more, then naturally, it would be a sure thing that the relationship would be set for the long run.

When you operate from this space, you can find yourself inadvertently trying to earn love by doing far too much. Subconsciously, you believe your worth lies in how much you can give. This automatically puts you in your masculine energy and forces the man out of his — trust me ladies, it is not sustainable, nor is it comfortable for a man who is a true leader and a provider. The men that are receptive to you doing all of the work will not be the same men who can confidently lead a household. A true leader and provider will allow you to sit in your feminine energy, so that you are not in a relationship where you are trying to play the role of both partners.

EXPLORING ATTACHMENT STYLES

As originally proposed by John Bowlby and further developed by Mary Ainsworth, attachment theory offers a powerful framework for understanding how your early relationships influence your approach to love. Now, even though we are not going to dive too much into the details of this, here are the four main attachment styles:

Secure Attachment: To put it simply, you are secure in yourself and in interpersonal relationships. You feel confident in relationships and trust that your partner will meet your needs, and if they don't, you have firm boundaries to leave if they are not met.

Anxious Attachment: You will know if this is your dominant attachment style because you will crave closeness but also simultaneously fear abandonment, often leading to clingy or overbearing behavior. Now all of us humans don't want to be abandoned, but this fear when that is your ruling attachment style doesn't just stop at a small thought of, "I hope this goes well because I really like this person."

It means that when there is a real or perceived threat of being abandoned, a deep core wound is triggered, and you may find yourself spiraling and overcompensating in order to avoid being abandoned by your partner in reality.

Dismissive Avoidant Attachment: You value independence to the point of pushing people away, fearing intimacy. Someone with this attachment style can normally be seen as someone who has been "chronically" single, if not for an extended period of their life, but maybe their entire life. Love can be seen as too hard to even entertain and that solitude is the preferred way of living and is somehow more "grown up."

If you do end up in any kind of connection, you usually will create so much distance that the other person is forced to chase you, making the relationship extremely one-sided until they finally give up — to your relief. Any kind of deep intimacy for you feels like you are being engulfed, and you are drowning.

Fearful-Avoidant Attachment: You oscillate between craving connection and fearing it, creating a push-pull dynamic. This is arguably the most painful attachment style to experience on both sides. When this is your attachment style, you are both the extreme versions of anxious and avoidant. When your anxious side is triggered, the pursuit of love is what drives you...rather better said, the "illusion of what love is." I refer to this as an illusion because when that is your dominant attachment style, you are driven to chase after the fantasy version of a relationship, the one that will soothe and finally heal your core wound — not the pursuit of having genuine and healthy love with the other person for who they are from a secure sense of self. It is why, when you or another person has this attachment style and avoidance is triggered, it can be a devastating experience.

The person with this attachment style will experience, what I like to call, almost "blacking out" or emotional deactivation as a reaction to what their brain understands as a totally necessary threat response. The "threat" could be any minor inconvenience in the relationship that triggers a core wound and forces a person with this attachment style to flee as if their life depended on it.

Neurologically, the emotional deactivation happens when the once lovey-dovey, borderline clingy person you or the other person once were appears to disappear overnight and the result is a stone-cold person to deal with instead who feels unrecognizable. Once deactivation has occurred, this person may have cutting words to say, if any words are exchanged at all, because silence is the most common weapon when avoidance is the main driver. This can often make the person on the receiving end of this feel like they are crazy because it feels like they are suddenly dealing with a complete stranger. However, what is even more interesting is that although it may never be apparent, the person doing the deactivating is in just as much emotional pain, if not more than the other person. This is because they know that they are the cause of the rupture, yet they find it too confronting to deal with themselves and so, running away and starting the cycle again further down the line with someone new is the best option for them.

Understanding your attachment style helps you identify triggers and patterns in your dating life. For instance, if you're anxiously attached, you might interpret a delayed text as rejection. If you're someone that gets triggered by someone who is openly trying to plan things with you for the relationship and this makes you recoil, despite there not being any real reason to, perhaps you may be avoidant. Recognizing this allows you to pause and respond from a place of self-awareness rather than insecurity. You get to own your attachment style from a place of power and start to position yourself in a healthier stance to enjoy the joys of being in a loving relationship that makes you feel safe and is actually good for you.

SELF-SABOTAGE: HOW UNHEALED WOUNDS AFFECT YOUR DATING LIFE

Self-sabotage doesn't always have to look so dramatic. Sometimes self-sabotage is as simple as ghosting someone because you're afraid they might hurt you first. Other times, it's staying in a talking stage with a man who shows no long-term intention, hoping he'll eventually change. These are the kind of men who have more fantasies about the future than a practical plan to actually make your shared dreams a reality.

JOURNAL PROMPT: *In order to heal, you must identify the root of these behaviors.*

Ask yourself: *What story am I telling myself about love? Is it one of scarcity, fear, or even unworthiness?*

I recommend really taking some time to work through these questions in order to benefit from this exercise, and also make it something you come back to when you do catch yourself in any of the patterns we have looked at in this chapter.

WHY HEALING IS FOUNDATIONAL TO ATTRACTING THE RIGHT PARTNER

Here's the truth (even if it sounds cliché): You don't attract what you want; you attract who you are and where you are on your journey. This isn't some woo-woo explanation; scientifically, we all vibrate at a certain frequency. This habitual pattern of blocking love either by overextending or by blocking it altogether and keeping it at arm's length because it's "scary," "a waste of time," or "dangerous," is a frequency at which emotional unavailability can thrive. That's why sometimes it can feel confusing if you feel that you are putting yourself out there and still only manage to attract men who seem like they cannot commit. The bottom line is that you are drawn to each other because you are two peas in the same pod. A man who flakes, can't commit, and is on some level evasive finds himself in your world, because he can sense that you two have an emotional capacity block. This translates as a perfect match because it feels safe for him. He knows that he isn't truly going to be challenged to change himself in the same way that a more securely attached person, who is not open for complication would be.

Let's go deeper into this type of man, briefly. If you are honest with yourself, what was the one thing or sometimes, few things that felt a little off to you about them even if they appeared good on paper at first? Was it the fact that they mentioned how successful they were, but you never once heard them mention an actual paying client? Perhaps it was that they apparently missed you so much but barely were able to lock down a date and time to meet as each week came and passed? Maybe it was the way they swore they were so into you and were ready to leave the dating apps for you, but in your presence, they kept their phone faced down? Whatever it is, there is usually a time when a woman can look back after the fact and notice that there was a micro slip in integrity because she felt that something was not quite right and she suppressed her intuition, regardless. And why was that? Why did you feel like having this person in your life and gaining their approval was more important than listening to the messages that your body was trying to tell you?

When you continue to do this work, your intrinsic value will be so deafening that you will no longer be able to suppress it from a place of micro-abandonment. Instead, you will get into the habit of witnessing with discernment, collecting the data and storing it for later to create a bigger picture of that person and their actions. By not getting caught up in the history of the red flags of the men of your romantic past or on the other side of the scale, falling head over heels with someone based on chemistry alone, deciphering what healthy love looks and feels like will slowly become a muscle you build. *Even if you have never had a healthy relationship before.* This is because when you date with a level of objectivity this allows you to safely be involved with someone where you offer a healthy dose of emotional connection whilst ensuring that you are regularly assessing whether or not the dynamic is a good fit for both of you. As you start to normalize peace and regular pace in all areas of your life in general, not just your love life, you'll be drawn to men who align with your core values and emotional needs — not the false self that you have created out of survival.

One thing that can happen when you have had bad experiences in love and dating is that feeling of failure that can start to chip away at your self-esteem. Without your self-awareness, you can start to internalize this as meaning something about your own ability to even tell a "good" person from a "bad" one. Does this sound familiar? First of all, there are no "bad" people or men. In order to profoundly heal, you will need to divorce yourself completely from this idea. There are, however, men whose core values do not align with yours — in some cases this is a temporary thing and maybe these evolve with time as they go through life on their own path. Perhaps their behavior as a result of this mismatch of values makes you construe that this is not a great way to treat people. The fact of the matter is that you have only had your life experience. What you really are saying is that their behavior is not how you want to be treated because it goes against your own core values. The "bad" part is if your brain is signaling the mismatch — but that is all it is — a mismatch — not an inherently bad person.

Without healing, even the best dating strategies will fall flat. That is something a lot of women are not ready to hear, but is the truth. None of what you see on social media or even in your personal life, where you see happy couples, is a result of just two people waking up perfect and finding each other by chance. What you don't see behind the photos and closed doors is the fact that relationships take collaborative work. Each individual, however, has to remember that their own inner work is their responsibility in order to contribute the best to the relationship.

Finding Strength in Healing

I remember one particular relationship that brought everything to the surface for me. He was probably at the time the most handsome man I had ever met, and he happened to say all the right things...or at least at first. He was a few years older than me. I would say maybe five to seven years older. But as time went on, he started to really drop the ball; initially with the little things and then eventually it turned into full-blown cold shoulder and disrespect. I ignored the subtle red flags, and I convinced myself that if I just tried harder, he would come around. Deep down, I was afraid to walk away because I believed leaving would mean starting over, and that just felt like failure. I had grown up never really planning my life further than five years at a time so at the very young age I was when I met a man like this, it truly felt like my entire world would be over if I left him because the distant future felt like a blur that I couldn't really visualize. People around me would say, "Oh, you have your whole life ahead of you," but I never saw life like that growing up and therefore made a lot of decisions based on this short-sighted vision I had.

One night, he disrespected me for the last time, and I'd had enough. I ended it very abruptly then and there but it's strange because any time when I was younger, and I left a man, it felt like I was the one who suffered more. It weirdly felt like I was the one getting abandoned even though I was the one doing the abandoning. Sadly, he wasn't the first man I'd allowed to treat me like an afterthought, and unless something changed, he wouldn't be the last. The common denominator wasn't them; it was the unhealed version of me who didn't believe she deserved more.

DATE YOUR WORTH, NOT YOUR WOUND

That night, I made a promise to myself: I would stop chasing love and start chasing healing. The journey wasn't linear or glamorous. Some days, it felt like progress; other days felt like I'd fallen back into old habits. But little by little, I began to recognize my worth. I started setting boundaries, not just with others, but with myself. I gave myself permission to say "no" to situations that felt draining and "yes" to experiences that nourished me. Slowly, I rebuilt my self-trust, one decision at a time. The most profound change came when I finally let go of the narrative that I needed someone else to complete me. Instead, I focused on becoming the best version of myself. And when I least expected it, love found me — not because I was looking for it, but because I was finally ready to receive it.

Healing your wounds isn't easy, but it's worth it. If I can do it, so can you. Start by giving yourself permission to feel, to let go, and to believe that you are deserving of the love you've always dreamed of.

CHAPTER

4

THE THREE CORE LOVE WOUNDS: ABANDONMENT WOUND

If you're reading this, I don't need to tell you that your childhood and past relationships have left wounds that shaped your dating patterns. You already know that. The reason they continue to play a huge part in what you experience in your dating life is that simply just acknowledging them isn't enough. Just like loving the "idea of love" isn't enough. Before we can get into what this really means, let's consider what the three most common love wounds are when it comes to dating:

ABANDONMENT WOUND

A typical sign of an abandonment wound is having a fear of being discarded. The root cause of this usually comes from an early childhood experience where love felt conditional or inconsistent on some level. For instance, perhaps you had a parent and/or caregiver whose behavior taught you that you could not just be loved for who you are, and for simply existing on the planet. They instead taught you to believe that you needed to earn their love either by actually proving yourself to them, or doing something special.

The abandonment wound is not only a fear of someone leaving you if you do not act as per how you *feel* they want you to, but it is simultaneously an abandonment of your true self. You end up morphing into what you think is going to result in external validation from another person by leaving behind your core self, and disconnecting with your own deeper needs.

In adulthood, this can look like clinging to unhealthy relationships and staying in dynamics much longer than you know you should. It can also look like over-investing too early, either with your own energy, financially, emotionally, or all of the above.

The key inner message that you are telling yourself is that, *as long as you do your part to "SAVE" the connection, you will never be left alone.* It is the belief that if you shrink yourself enough into the shape and size that causes the other person the least discomfort, that is when you will be appreciated. What happens usually is exactly what you hoped wouldn't happen.

The abandonment wound feels like you can take control over it by being as little of a perceived nuisance to your (potential) partner as possible. However, think about it...what kind of energy do you think this level of intense surrender of your personal needs projects? Ironically, it is not the kind of magnetic energy that will magically make someone stay with you.

It provokes the other person to unconsciously respect you less — sometimes over time, sometimes immediately.

At our core, when you strip away all the layers of modern living and capitalist conditioning, we are still animals wired for survival. On a primal level, people instinctively evaluate whether someone can care for themselves and others, not only through strength and stability, but also through emotional intelligence and self-awareness. So when someone sees that you're willing to completely empty your cup for them, it triggers two subconscious messages:

A) **You don't value yourself enough, which makes it harder for them to see your worth through their own eyes, and**

B) **You're neglecting the most basic survival principle of putting yourself first, which can lead them to question whether you're capable of taking care of them, or even of a family, in the long run.**

Deep down, if you are reading this book, you are not the kind of person looking for a short-term relationship; otherwise, why would you need to read this, right? You are looking for profound, lasting love, and leading with an abandonment wound is not going to allow that kind of connection in. Operating from this wound long term will have you chasing people who just simply do not have the capacity for the love that you are looking for, and perhaps they never will.

This is a particular wound where there is no such thing as fully healing it. It will always be there; in fact, dare I say that this is true about our core wounds in general. They are not in our lives for us to heal — *one and done* — so that we can move on and live life perfectly afterwards. Each of your core wounds serve as lessons for you and are lifelong reminders. They are there to give you a reality check every time that you go slightly off balance, to tell you, "Hey, this is too far from your emotional security edge — pick a safer, balanced, and more grounded route."

Your mission if this is your core wound, is to build your own inner security. You master this by constantly reminding yourself that you're whole and worthy, regardless of anyone else's actions.

The abandonment wound thrives in your life as a result of you telling yourself that someone is somehow "better than you." By positioning them as better than you, you simultaneously tell yourself that there is no room for you to also be of high value. Have you ever seen two gold medalists share the same level of the podium when they win a game? Never, right? Now, in actual real life, it can happen on rare occasions, and I believe only for specific games — but the general RULE? One gold medalist. That gold medalist winner is supposed to be you — not a man who barely provides you with the bare minimum and whose personality is mainly a fabrication of the idealized one you are projecting on to him.

By coming back to yourself and remembering that your core needs are an intrinsic part of who you are, putting someone else repeatedly before yourself no longer becomes your default behavior.

The unspoken truth about the abandonment wound is that this is a covert way of manipulating the other person. By showing up as "perfect," that is to say, someone who has no problem bending over backwards for someone else with little thought about their own needs, **you are not demonstrating that you are real and authentic.** You are wearing a mask and showing up as the person you think everyone wants to see. There is truly nothing honest about this, and this is done in order to make the person you want to attract act in a certain way for your own benefit; i.e. *if I am doing all of this for you, I want love in return.*

So yes, I know that this is hard to hear, but this is a form of emotional coercion even if you don't mean it to be. Seeing those words on this page might be deeply triggering, but it is part of the wake-up call needed to realize that you cannot continue to operate in this way if you truly want to attract a soulmate partnership moving forward.

In order to assess whether this is your dominant core love wound, use the following journal prompts below:

Abandonment Wound Self Reflection

1. When someone I care about becomes distant, how do I usually react, and what story do I tell myself about what their distance means?

2. What emotions do I feel when I don't hear back from someone I'm dating right away?

3. Do I tend to overextend myself (emotionally, physically, financially) to keep people close? Why?

4. When was the first time I remember feeling like someone important to me left (emotionally or physically), and how did I make sense of that as a child?

5. What do I fear would happen if I stopped chasing love and allowed it to come to me instead?

CHAPTER 5

THE THREE CORE LOVE WOUNDS: UNWORTHINESS WOUND

The unworthiness wound is highly served by the idea that there is only so much available for someone like you. It is the belief that because you have invested so much energy into pushing forward with your achievements that you have missed the boat when it comes to love, and you are somehow left with the dregs of the dating pool. You may have had instances where, because this belief feels so true for you, you have told yourself at some point that you may as well have *any* man because it is better than having no man at all.

This can rear its ugly head in many ways. Women that I have worked with who previously were married, and then ended up filing for divorce shortly afterward, often confess that they knew exactly why their marriage ended so fast. They often say that it was because they were aware from the beginning that they were suppressing their deeper desires for what they actually wanted in a relationship. Time and again, they admit that they forfeited this because they believed that the man in front of them was as good as it was going to get.

A lot of this sense of unworthiness can stem from experiences in childhood, where in some way you were told that you were too much or that you asked for too much. This can then be internalized into adulthood where you subconsciously convince yourself that you need to settle for less, in order to avoid rocking the boat. This is very characteristic if you had an experience in childhood where you were parentified, i.e. you were involuntarily placed in the parent role well before your years, and you accepted this role out of survival to perpetually keep the peace at all costs. Of course, in adult interpersonal relationships this can result in a deafening of your own intuition and inner voice. It can result in your choosing of partners that on some level, you believe will soothe a part of yourself that was lost in your childhood but at the same time, whilst bypassing what you now need as an adult.

Take one of my past relationships for example, where I can say I was in a beautiful, mutually loving connection, but I realized over time that it was becoming misaligned. I identified that I was actually choosing this person from the fantasy of the future family I wanted to create with them. They had grown up in a household full of so much love — MUCH more than I ever had a chance to experience in my own life growing up. I therefore subconsciously chose them in an attempt to heal that unworthiness wound from my past. I saw how easy it was for their family to pour into each other; the joy they brought to each other on every call or in-person meet ups without having to have *earned* that joy, was something I craved for my inner child and my future children to have. This wound can have you thinking that sacrificing your needs is what it takes to have pure love, when that couldn't be further from the truth.

In my experience, the voice I had been pushing down grew louder and louder, until I was faced with a crossroads situation in which I had a decision to make. I had two choices: either continue to suppress this voice for the rest of my life to maintain a relationship that, while not toxic, wasn't truly fulfilling my deepest desires. Or I could make a break for it and finally give myself the chance to have my needs met elsewhere.

There is something about settling that nobody ever really talks about. You hear the term "settling for less" and automatically the thought that comes to mind is someone abusive or someone blatantly not at your standard, but it can look a lot more subtle than that. **You can have a healthy relationship with a non-toxic person and still be settling.** Settling in this sense means deciding that you are staying in a relationship because it is what romantic abundance *should* look like, but in actual fact, it doesn't ring true for *you.*

This wound can also show up in a similar way to the abandonment wound. You do not want to be abandoned by the other person, so you do whatever it takes to save the relationship. With this wound, you will find yourself doing far too much to disguise the fact that there are cracks in the relationship. When this wound is active, you find yourself having this inexplicable desire to gain external validation, and not just once or twice, but on a consistent basis. This again is a covert mechanism that your psyche uses to try and gain other people's approval. In other words, if everyone else floods you with positive feedback about your relationship, then that can be enough to keep you in it. You are effectively "ticking all of society's boxes." You're not an alien because you have physical evidence that you are lovable, and therefore there is nothing wrong with you.

Overcompensating is another huge sign that the unworthiness wound has manifested in your adult life. Sometimes this can look like being both partners in a relationship when the truth is that, in reality, it doesn't actually feel like the other person you are with is 100% fulfilling their role. I have seen this in women sending themselves flowers in an attempt to either make their partner jealous or make everyone else watching think they have the kind of partner who shows affection in this way.

Overcompensating can also look like constantly being in battle mode when it comes to talking about your significant other with other people. In my experience, if every conversation results in you having to defend your partner's behavior, there is something monumentally wrong at the foundation of the relationship. Going into survival mode each time you are threatened by someone holding up a mirror to what is a clear imbalance in your relationship, is the breeding ground for not only a constantly dysregulated nervous system, but it is also encouraging inflammation to manifest in your precious body as well. The pre-emptive stress and panic that comes with having to reassure people that your partner is a good person, and that your relationship is fine, demonstrate that this is not a viable long-term plan. In the end, it usually comes at the cost of your own health.

It is hard not to talk about having a lack of deservingness without discussing the pattern of choosing a partner who displays consistent examples of being under equipped to provide you with a balanced relationship. These are the kind of partners where, on their part, it is mostly "take," and you are often left feeling empty-handed. The tricky part about this is that if you are in this scenario, it is likely that you have sacrificed your needs because this person meets criteria that you think is so rare and hard to come by. You may feel that the relationship exists solely based off of some sort of fluke luck and deep down, you are scared they will wake up one day and change their mind about you. Due to this perception of them or this specific quality they possess that you feel is so sought after, you psychologically render them as "limited edition," and therefore even when they show you they can hardly give you the bare minimum, you stay with them regardless.

In this dynamic, it is inconceivable for someone with a stable, secure attachment style to stay in this kind of relationship and remain content. If you have been in this situation, then you know that there are only two options available:

Option One: Run as far away from them as you can and preserve your sanity or,

Option Two: Stay with this person because you really believe there is nothing better out there...and watch the happy soul you once were become unrecognizable.

This wound is also dangerous because it can leave you wide...and I mean WIDE open to deeply controlling men. The scariest thing about controlling men is that by the time you meet them, it is usually not their first rodeo. They have been there and done that, and with each of their victims, they have learned to perfect their craft to such an extent that you can slowly find yourself experiencing, what psychologists call, the 'boiling frog syndrome'. What this means is that despite you being the intelligent and discerning person you are, you miss these red, and sometimes big crimson, flags all because they are not overtly obvious controlling behavior traits. In fact, your wound is so activated in this scenario, that you will find yourself readily quietening your intuition just as a way to self-soothe and avoid conflict.

When faced with controlling men, this wound will allow them to strategically pick apart your core values and disguise this as love when really it is about manipulation. As the cycle of self-abandonment continues to operate in this dynamic, you will find yourself allowing this kind of partner to slowly mold you into what *their* version of perfection is — the danger here is that this person is ALSO operating from their own core wounds. This therefore means that no amount of alterations to your core beliefs, personality, the way you socialize, dress, speak, etc. will *ever* be enough to satiate their need to project their own dissatisfaction with themselves onto you.

For those of you who have experienced this and escaped early, congratulations. Not every woman does. Many women will stay in these traps for years and years, only to end up with the very outcome they thought that morphing into what their partner wanted would prevent...being left for someone else. To these kind of men, once you conform to their twisted version of reality and completely become a puppet for them, they get bored. You are no longer a shiny, new challenge for them and so they move on to someone else to restart the cycle that gives them the dark dopamine hit they crave. Women who have suffered years of shrinking to avoid conflict with their controlling partners are usually walking ghosts of who they once were.

What is very rarely discussed is that no real man of high value would ever truly expect his woman to shrink for him. This need for you to be smaller and "under his thumb" is his avoidance strategy so that he doesn't have to look himself in the mirror, and deal with his own personal baggage. It is much easier to bully your bright and beautiful self into a corner so that at least in his own home, he can feel like the king of the castle. As this is not a practical solution, the level of control increases over time because his ego requires more proof that he is the number one, authoritarian alpha figure in your life. Before you know it, the woman you once were: ambitious, bubbly, adventurous — she will be asking a man, who doesn't deserve her, for permission to simply breathe.

The solution for this wound, like the other wounds, is straightforward. Reframe your worth entirely. I know that love is beautiful, and it can feel like the most special thing in the entire world...but it can also remove all of your senses because it is *that* powerful.

Your achievements are not and should never be a burden; they're a blessing. In fact, I have a list of all my life achievements in the notes section in my phone so that when I second-guess myself for a moment in any life scenario, I go to this part of my phone so I regularly remember *who the f*** I am*. Don't get me wrong, these are not just things like "I wrote a book" or, "I own a business." On my list are things like, "I had no real example of healthy love and I experienced it anyway." These are the things that, even though they don't have obvious tangible results, still weigh just as heavy, if not heavier, than what society says is a big achievement worth bragging about.

Everything that you have managed to move through and pick yourself up from makes you who you are. That special, fiery individual who is courageously reading this book to uncover yet another layer of herself... she is pure magic.

This is part of yourself that has to be tapped into on a daily basis so that you do not end up falling for either one of the extremes on the scale of having a partner who is not on your level — whether that is ending up with someone who is clearly abusive, dependent, or just simply not aligned with what you truly want. The right partner will celebrate all of your wins *alongside you* — not from below you because you are the big conqueror in the relationship, and not above you, towering over your accomplishments in an attempt to take you off your pedestal.

In order to assess whether this is your dominant core love wound, use the following journal prompts below:

Unworthiness Wound Self Reflection

1. When someone treats me well, do I find it easy or uncomfortable to receive that level of care?

2. In what ways do I still seek validation or approval to feel lovable or "good enough"?

3. How often do I downplay my needs, achievements, or desires so that others feel more comfortable around me?

4. If I fully believed I was worthy of unconditional love, what boundaries or standards would instantly change in my life?

5. What version of myself do I hide because I'm scared it might be "too much" or "not enough" for someone else?

CHAPTER 6

THE THREE CORE LOVE WOUNDS: CONTROL WOUND

The control wound is about having a deep fear of betrayal at a very young age. In your early years, something traumatic enough may have happened either directly to you, someone close to you, or your environment was deemed unsafe. Whatever the case was, you were powerless to stop anything bad from happening. This experience planted the seed in your mind that that was the weakest you have ever been in your life and that, whatever the outcome of that event was, had you been stronger, you could have prevented it from happening. It is an incredible amount of pressure to put on oneself, and the belief that you could have been the savior is often an untrue and unfair statement. It takes away the responsibility of the adults who were involved in the situation who should have been there to make the environment safer and/or less traumatic than it was.

This wound strengthens if, for example, you had any parents or caregivers who were aware of this particular event or series of events. Perhaps they either gaslit you into thinking the situation wasn't so bad or that somehow you contributed to it, despite it being unfeasible for you to have been able to at the time. It is a projection of their own sense of responsibility onto you so that they do not have to process the fact that they failed to protect you.

So many women that I work with have this experience and can often relate when I provide them with this example. When you learn to default to survival mode at such a young age, this habitual move can come with you into adulthood as you have enough evidence that it worked as a sufficient shield whilst growing up. In childhood, the control wound could have manifested as always wanting to be the lead, micromanaging tasks amongst your peers, having issues with being told what to do and finding it hard to let anyone really see the real you.

In adult relationships, the same patterns can be seen when you find yourself, for example, leading in the relationship with a man and fully taking on the masculine role. This is sometimes because you have little to no faith in their ability to fulfill that role. In theory, if he cannot have power over you or hurt you, then he has less chance of making you feel as defenseless as you did when you were a child. You may hear yourself saying in relationships, "If I want something done right around here, I will have to do it myself." It is a form of self-protection that you feel will help you avoid being disappointed by the other person; however, you do not realize that all of this power play kills intimacy.

DATE YOUR WORTH, NOT YOUR WOUND

When you constantly step into this role over and over again, one of two outcomes is possible with a man. He will either a) enjoy this, because it means that you are essentially mothering him and all he has to do is receive and never have to really assert himself at all, or b) a man who wants to lead and be in his masculinity will find this very uncomfortable, and will address this so it can change, or he will leave the relationship. The latter kind of man is the man I know you actually want; otherwise, you would not be reading this book.

So how do you get ahead of this wound? Simply learn how to fully embrace and step into your feminine energy without fear. Trust that being present, receptive, and authentic is enough...because it is. There is power in being soft and strong; they do not have to be antonyms. And for some of you, you may be rolling your eyes thinking that I am not making any sense, but years ago I would have agreed with you.

Years ago, I too thought I had to power through life in this masculine energy to stay alive and be respected. I did that until I had my first burnout experience and realized that this was just not sustainable for me as a woman long term. My soul begged for me to connect with my true feminine essence, particularly when it came to my relationships. I was so done with taking care of everyone around me growing up, walking on eggshells trying not to bruise fragile egos, and I was exhausted from it. And I am sure you are too.

In order to assess whether this is your dominant core love wound, use the following journal prompts below:

Control Wound Self Reflection

1. When I feel uncertain in love, do I try to manage the situation, and what do I believe that control will protect me from?

2. How do I react when someone challenges my perspective or tries to take the lead in a relationship?

3. What parts of myself feel unsafe when I'm not the one in charge or "holding it all together"?

4. When did I first learn that being in control made me feel safe, and what was happening in my environment at that time?

5. What would "surrender" in love look like to me, and what emotions arise when I imagine that?

BONUS TRAINING

HEALING THE THREE LOVE WOUNDS: HOW TO END EMOTIONALLY UNAVAILABLE CYCLES FOR GOOD

Now that you've explored the **three core love wounds** (abandonment, unworthiness, and control), it's time to go deeper. In the **Healing the Three Love Wounds** training, we'll move beyond awareness into *embodiment and transformation,* helping you shift the patterns that have been keeping you stuck in love.

In this training, you'll discover:

- A deeper understanding of each core wound: how they form, how they show up in your emotional landscape, and how to begin softening its hold on your relationships.

- The link between your nervous system, attachment style, and emotional responses, so you can move from reaction to regulation.

- A practical tool to begin rewiring old patterns and open yourself to love that feels deeply fulfilling.

HOW TO ACCESS YOUR BONUS TRAINING

1. **Go to** https://www.rachelroseonline.com/ .

2. **Select "Video Trainings."**

3. **Select the relevant training for this chapter and use code "YOUAREWORTHY" at checkout for free access.**

CHAPTER 7

TRUST: THE FOUNDATION OF LASTING LOVE

Trust. This is genuinely the silent thread that holds every healthy, lasting relationship together. It is the currency of love and emotional safety. Sadly, the concept of trust for you, someone who desires to meet her soulmate, may feel like the most elusive or fragile thing on the planet right now. Why is that? Well, like I have stated earlier, strong, ridiculously ambitious women are forged in fire. Often that fire involves experiencing extreme betrayal, heartbreak, abandonment, or repeated disappointments in love. As a result, rebuilding trust may feel almost impossible. And what happens when multiple women across the globe have similar experiences and a smartphone? They take to social media and amplify the problem to the point where it feels like an epidemic. It can sometimes feel like it is a mystery that literally anyone is ever able to trust another human walking behind them down the road, let alone in a full-blown relationship.

It's interesting when you look deeper at this because it is likely that you learned to trust yourself in your career moves and in close friendships, but when it comes to men and romantic relationships, there is a wall. It is as if there is a lingering doubt, a quiet voice inside whispering, "Can I really trust again?"

This chapter is here to help you answer that question, because the truth is, trust is not something you find in someone else. *It is something you build within yourself first, and not enough people are talking about this.*

WHY TRUST IS THE BEDROCK OF LOVE

Without trust, love cannot breathe. You cannot build a genuine connection with real emotional intimacy if you are chronically bracing for disappointment. This isn't just some passing comment or a woo-woo belief. It is based on the science that staying in hypervigilance means that you are less receptive to the kind of gentle, real love trying to get in because your brain perceives closeness in general as a threat; whether it actually is or not.

The loss of trust is often layered in multiple different flavors of being let down by someone you held very highly and trusted. More often than not, their change in behavior and/or actions completely blindsided you. Acknowledging this part, though, is part of your healing. The second that you place whatever wound you have, whether it is betrayal or any of the other core wounds discussed in the previous chapters under a microscope, you automatically take away its power. At the end of the day, the threat that the brain is responding to only has as much power as you feed it. When you cut off its supply by dissecting what is really behind your fear, you are already 20 steps ahead of the game in dismantling the beliefs that are keeping you from being able to establish a fundamental part of a safe relationship.

These wounds can create unconscious patterns that can last an entire lifetime. I have met countless women who are drop-dead gorgeous, financially stable, well educated, etc. These are the kind of women where you would have to be blind not to see they were catches, and yet many of them have been single for a decade or even longer. Staying in the trauma of betrayal can be such a lifelong sentence of loneliness without you even realizing it. This is because it creates a subconscious loop in your mind where you are constantly "waiting for the other shoe to drop," *even with good, emotionally available men who are eager and intentional.* The hard truth that I am so happy I get to give you today is this: **you cannot receive healthy love if you don't believe it exists.**

REBUILDING SELF-TRUST

One of the most profound effects of emotional wounds is the erosion of self-trust. When a past relationship ends in betrayal or heartbreak, it's easy to blame yourself: "I should have seen the red flags." Over time, this self-doubt makes it harder to trust your instincts, leaving you vulnerable to repeating the same mistakes. This can also contribute to the building of a barrier seen in some of the ways you can auto-self protect/overcompensate when it comes to love by adopting an insecure attachment style.

Rebuilding self-trust involves letting go of the guilt or shame associated with past decisions. It may feel counter-intuitive at first; however, forgiving yourself is the first step towards experiencing love in a completely different way. *You did the best you could with the knowledge you had at the time.* That may sound cliché, but it is ultimately true. You are not fighting a fair battle with yourself, telling yourself that you should have seen the signs you missed, now that you have more information about why a relationship ended. I feel that women who have achieved so much often forget just how intelligent and intuitive they actually are, the second that a love relationship does not work out as planned.

I also find in general there is a heavy attachment when it comes to relationships only being successful if they are long term. All relationships are valuable — short and long term. When you see each person that you become romantically involved with as a divine messenger sent by whichever higher power you believe in, be it the Universe, God, the angels, etc. you start to understand that every connection is a learning experience. Even the ones that may not be the most comfortable. Repeated cycles are not punishment, nor are they proof that you are inherently "bad at love." They are just messages to confirm that your current strategy is making you feel less than your best self. They serve as reminders to show you that in order to experience love differently, you need to not only show up differently, but understand it differently. This doesn't need to be an overnight shift; however, you can start by taking baby steps by just speaking to yourself with a little more kindness than you did yesterday. Treat yourself as you would a close friend a little more each day. This is how you create steady and lasting change without completely overwhelming your nervous system and triggering imposter syndrome.

My Personal Story: Rebuilding Trust After Betrayal

One relationship, in particular, left a mark on me when it comes to betrayal. I had let my guard down with someone who, in the beginning, seemed to check every box. He was charismatic, successful, and emotionally expressive. But slowly, I began to see cracks. Inconsistencies. Moments when my gut told me something was off, but I ignored it, chalking it up to my own overthinking. He was a big self-sabotager, and it ended with me leaving him and me moving to another country as part of my undergraduate degree.

I kid you not that post-break up, it felt like half a breath later, he was in a full-blown relationship with someone he had been calling his "friend" the entire time we were supposed to be committed to each other. Oh, and get this...I spent a YEAR of my life, ladies, with no girlfriend title, only for this man to put WIFE in capital letters all over social media, along with post after post about him and his wonderful, new relationship. You cannot make this stuff up. He never admitted to cheating, but come on...the writing was very much on the wall here! When the betrayal finally came to light, it wasn't just about him. It shattered my trust in myself. I couldn't stop thinking:

"How did I not see this?"
"Why did I ignore the red flags?"
"How can I ever trust myself to choose a man again?"

It definitely changed me whilst I was living in another country to someone a lot more callous when it came to men, and therefore my experience with them was just as non-committal for over two years. I was open to meeting men, but I was notorious for not letting them all the way in emotionally. I stayed emotionally guarded. I kept one foot out the door at all times, rehearsing my exit strategy in case they let me down. It wasn't until I did the real work of rebuilding trust from within that everything shifted. I learned how to:

- Listen to my intuition without overthinking.

- Hold space for my vulnerability without self-judgment.

- Release the belief that all men would eventually disappoint me.

Once I had moved back to London, I finally experienced my first real, long-term relationship. Like my first ever non-on-again, off-again type of relationship, to the point where we both felt we would want to marry each other. When I finally re-established trust with myself, love showed up effortlessly. Not because the world changed, but because I changed the way I related to love.

What's so special about this turning point is that with each serious relationship, but especially from that particular relationship onwards, I had a new energetic standard for love and for myself. And yes, there was always uncharted territory in different dynamics, but I was challenging myself with baby steps. Like, "Yes, you can do this. It doesn't matter what your childhood looked like or that you had no example of what safe love looks like…just wing it, because you've got your own back, and that's more than enough."

The following pillars are what solidified a core part of how I was able to radically change the way I was able to navigate and sustain relationships moving forward; even when it felt completely scary and like I was absolutely faking my belief that this could actually work:

THE THREE PILLARS OF TRUST

1. Trust in Yourself

This is the most foundational piece. If you do not trust yourself to make good decisions, enforce boundaries, and walk away from what is misaligned, you will always feel unsafe in love. There is no greater compass than your own inner knowing. You already have the answers, it is just a question of turning up the volume on the voice inside of you that knows what truly makes you happy, and what choices will lead you to repeat past patterns that no longer serve you.

2. Trust in Men

This is where many women get stuck. When you've been deeply hurt, it feels safer to believe that men can't be trusted. You are required to be brave and deeply forgiving of both yourself and others who have hurt you in the past. This is the only way to reignite your passion that was once lit for men, and rewire the brain to get excited again about all the great qualities a genuine and healthy partner can bring to a relationship.

3. Trust in the Process

Love doesn't always arrive on your desired timeline. Trusting the process means releasing the need to force commitment and believing that the right relationship is on its way to you. As much as I adore the kind of go-getter woman that you are, you are admittedly a control freak when it comes to this! Remind yourself of how well things have always managed to turn out for you so far in other areas of your life. Perhaps you always end up landing a new job just at the right time. Maybe you are someone who receives money magically out of nowhere just when a hefty, unexpected bill arrives. It could be that you always attract incredibly serendipitous opportunities...the kind that leave others wondering how on Earth you were able to manifest them, without even trying. Channel *that* energy into your love life and watch your experience transform, almost overnight.

HEALING STARTS WITH YOU

The journey to rebuilding trust is not about finding someone who will never hurt you. It's about becoming a woman who trusts herself so deeply that she knows she can handle whatever life brings. When you trust yourself, you will be able to engage in dating and relationships again, because you know that you will not abandon yourself for someone else like you have done in the past. You will walk away quickly from what is misaligned. You will receive healthy love with ease, because the inner knowing that you are always there to support yourself means that you don't outsource that feeling to anyone else. Essentially, anything that feels like chaos will feel like something you are allergic to.

And lastly, because you know that ultimately, you are in the driving seat sitting in your feminine power, you no longer need to manage the relationship. Even if you meet someone who tries to control and dominate you, you will not mistake this for love because it will feel in complete juxtaposition to the peace that you cultivate within yourself.

PART TWO: JOURNAL REFLECTIONS AND AFFIRMATIONS

Healing isn't about fixing yourself — it's about remembering your wholeness. It's peeling back the layers of protection you built to survive and letting love in again, safely this time. This part of your journey requires compassion, forgiveness, and softness — qualities that may have felt unsafe before, but are essential for expansion.

PROMPTS:

1. **Emotional Completion**
   What moments from your past still live rent-free in your heart?
   What experiences still feel emotionally unfinished, and what would bring me closure?

2. **Emotional Reactions**
   Healing means understanding your reactions, not judging them.
   How do I usually respond when I feel unseen, unsafe, or rejected in relationships?

3. **Identifying Wounds**
   The first step in healing is naming the pain.
   Which core love wound — abandonment, unworthiness,

or control — *feels most active right now, and how does it shape my choices?*

4. **Meeting Triggers with Compassion**
   Your triggers are simply invitations for self-compassion.
   How can I respond with curiosity and care instead of shame when I'm triggered?

5. **Releasing Old Identities**
   Every new chapter requires letting go of an old version of yourself.
   Who am I finally ready to release with love, and who am I ready to become?

PART THREE: EMBODIMENT

"Your energy is the invitation but your standards, however, are the filter." — *Rachel Rose*

CHAPTER

8

REDEFINING LOVE FOR THE MODERN WOMAN

What does love mean to you? It wouldn't surprise me if, when you ask yourself this question, the answer feels complicated. Somewhere along the way, you were taught that love looked a certain way: traditional, dependent, maybe even restrictive if this mirrors your parents' style when raising you. And for many of us, that narrative never felt right.

In this chapter, we are going to dismantle the outdated stories and societal expectations around love. You will learn how to redefine love on your own terms, one that complements your ambition, honors your standards, and allows you to create a deeply fulfilling partnership without feeling like you are obliged to live according to a specific timeline. This is why some women feel so overwhelmed when it comes to relationships nowadays, and choose not to bother at all, letting life pass them by without ever experiencing lasting love. And it is so understandable why. It can seem like there is an overwhelmingly high expectation to live a specific way, along with social media in your face spreading lies that love is dead and promoting feminine hyper-independence. Not to mention the "experts" giving you hollow advice that centers around what I like to call, soft prostitution, by only allowing men to date to you if they send you money via bank transfers or money transfer apps (ew). We are surrounded by this kind of content, and so I do not blame you for sometimes feeling like you are done with love.

LOVE IS A DOING WORD

One of the hardest lessons I've learned is that most people believe love is just a feeling — a soft, beautiful emotion that happens when we find the "right" person. We grow up thinking that love is the flutter in your chest, the butterflies, the spark, the rush of chemistry. And while those things are undeniably a part of love, they're not the foundation of it.

Real, genuine love is so much more. Love isn't just a noun — it's a verb. It's not something you *have*, it's something you *do*. Without the doing, what we call "love" often becomes a thousand other things: infatuation, desire, admiration, comfort, control, or attachment. But pure love, the kind that expands you, is active. It's alive. It's how you show up when it's inconvenient, how you listen when it would be easier to walk away, how you nurture a connection instead of expecting it to maintain itself.

Love is choosing yourself and the other person, over and over again. It's choosing someone not only in their brightest moments but also when they can't meet you perfectly in every moment. It's remembering that connection isn't about perfection; it's about presence.

The truth is, genuine love requires a level of maturity that most people don't realize they need until they're tested. It's easy to love when everything feels effortless. It's far harder when life demands patience, compassion, and deep emotional intelligence.

That's when love becomes a mirror. Because to truly love someone, you must first have reached a certain capacity within yourself: an emotional and spiritual bandwidth that allows you to hold space for another without losing yourself in the process. If you haven't built that capacity, love can feel threatening. It will expose your insecurities, highlight your wounds, and challenge your sense of control.

That's why self-love isn't just a catchy phrase; it's the prerequisite for healthy relationships. The love you give to yourself sets the tone for every other love you allow into your life. When you treat yourself with respect, kindness, and grace, you begin to expect and attract people who do the same. When you neglect yourself, you unconsciously invite relationships that mirror that neglect.

Love, in its truest form, is both giving and grounded. It's not about losing yourself in someone else's story. It's about two people walking side by side, both whole and both willing to pour into each other from fullness. It's also not about constant harmony. Real love has friction. It has depth and it inevitably invites growth. There will be moments when you clash and when your old wounds rise to the surface. But even then, love is not about fixing or forcing; it's about staying curious. It's about saying, *"I want to understand you, even when I don't agree with you."* When you see love this way, you begin to realize that it's not fragile at all — it's the most resilient force on the planet. It endures not because it's perfect, but because it's intentional.

Dare I say that perhaps one of the greatest acts of love is also knowing when to let go with grace. When to recognize that the most loving thing you can do for someone, or for yourself, is to release what no longer serves your highest good.

So when I say that love is a doing word, I mean that it's a conscious practice. It's in how we show up for ourselves first, so that when we meet someone else, we are not asking them to fill a void, but to join us in expansion in order to navigate the world together as a team.

WHY YOU NEED TO REDEFINE LOVE

I know the pressure is real, and you are bombarded with both correct and incorrect ways to do love, but this is the very reason why you need to redefine love on your own terms as a priority. Remember that people show you only what they want you to see.

Monogamy may not be for you. Marriage may not be for you. Children may not be for you. And it's all OK! Learning how to have standards that you do not have to apologize for is a huge step towards building the love life of your dreams that not enough people are focusing on. It truly doesn't need to look like everyone else's version. You need to remember that you are only seeing a very small, curated version of everyone's partnership... *and things are rarely ever as they seem.*

Let's look at some examples of couples doing things *their way*:

EXAMPLE A: I know of couples that have been together for years, but have an open relationship where, as long as they are together when it happens, they are allowed to add third parties into the mix to spice up their lives in the bedroom — *you would never know that just by looking at them.*

EXAMPLE B: I know of another married couple who don't even share the same room in their house, and sometimes they spend ample time...I am talking months at a time...in the same city but in different places entirely, and it works for them.

EXAMPLE C: I know of other couples where they have completely different religions, and instead of pressuring each other to drop their beliefs for the other person, they raise their child in a multi-faith household. This is to allow their child to experience both religions and then decide what path aligns for them most when they reach adulthood.

EXAMPLE D: I know of a handful of couples now who want to stay eternally engaged and never want to actually be legally married to one another. For them, the promise of forever is what is the most important thing, and they do not want the legal implications of traditional marriage.

Nobody is shouting any of these kinds of special conditions from the rooftop because quite frankly, it is nobody's business what happens behind closed doors in any given couple's private life. *So why do you hand over so much power to everyone else when it comes to what love needs to look like for you?*

My motto for life is this: **Do what you want first, and then tell people once it's done.** Forget about asking for permission or validation for your own personal choices. The more you teach the people in your life that you are an autonomous adult that makes executive decisions for themselves, the more people respect that even if they do share their opinion on what they feel is best for you, ultimately it is *you* who will be deciding how your life is run on your terms. Anyone in your life who doesn't understand this concept is thinking more about themselves, and they are likely projecting their own unprocessed emotions on to you. There is no need to feel bad or contort your desires when it comes to something as deeply personal as the style of relationship that is going to fulfill you.

My main advice in this chapter comes down to protecting your peace and sovereignty at all costs. Real, genuine love will not require you to sacrifice your dreams in order to keep the relationship afloat. I remember when I was in one relationship where we swore neither of us would suddenly apply to a job in another city, even if we really wanted to, because it would be unfair on the other person. I realize in hindsight how codependent that was because, *why shouldn't the other person get to explore a new environment?*

Love is not ownership. It is a partnership. It is two people deciding to choose each other over and over again. Part of your redefinition of love, in my opinion, needs to be through the lens of healthy detachment — you do not possess the other person. This belief alone will set you free in so many ways, and may actually be the catalyst for some of the deepest loves you will experience during your time on the planet. When love is not given excessive restriction, it thrives so much because you are allowing each other to fully bloom into the fullest expression of yourselves, uncapping the potential of what each of you could truly become. Trying to hold on to your person for dear life whether they are in the same room with you, or halfway across the world, is not about love at all. If this occurs, there is ultimately a deeper issue at play, because if the relationship is stable and both of your emotional needs are fulfilled, then there is very little that can break that down.

Part of the healthy detachment which will provide you with relationships that thrive more than any romantic dynamic you have ever experienced, is understanding that whilst relationships are powerful messengers that come into our lives; they all have an ending. This happens either through the end of human life or separation — they are the only options, and one of them is inevitable. That isn't to put a damper on looking for a relationship in the first place, of course, but it should help you see that we as humans are not going to be here forever.

We all have a set purpose and a precious amount of time to heal, grow, and make an impact in the world. And whilst doing that, we get to do it in a loving partnership, which helps us reach our next level of greatness in the process. That being said, we are each fragile and should be handled with care. We are all also in each other's lives for an infinite amount of reasons that only God/ the angels/ the Universe know why.

Redefining love will involve changing your relationship with love itself. When we experience love, what we are saying to the higher powers that be is that we are open to receiving the lessons at hand, no matter how long, short, painful, joyous, etc. We do not discriminate, because we have the inner trust that no matter what happens, we will make it through. We put our faith in the belief that every experience in each partnership will have the insights to make us stronger, and push us closer towards our Earthly purpose.

DATE YOUR WORTH, NOT YOUR WOUND

The Modern Love Paradigm

In the modern paradigm of love, you get to choose a partnership that:

- Enhances your life, rather than consumes it.
- Supports your goals, rather than competes with them.
- Feels expansive, not restrictive.

It requires unlearning everything you were taught about love and re-imagining what it looks like when you get to define it on your terms.

Your Unique Vision of Love

Redefining love begins with clarity. What does love look and feel like for you? Here are some powerful journal prompts to help you define your own love blueprint:

1. What outdated beliefs about love are you ready to release?
2. How do you want to feel in your ideal relationship?
3. What qualities and values are non-negotiable for your next partner?
4. How can your ambition and relationship thrive together in the future?
5. What are your personal standards for love, and how can you honor them daily?

This is your invitation to move from default settings to conscious creation in your love life.

CHAPTER 9

THE STANDARDS RESET

I have to start this chapter with something hilarious that I saw on social media. It must be my algorithm. Of course, as a Relationship Coach I get all sorts of memes, posts, and reels all related to relationships, but I truly get the amazing, the questionable, and the ugly. Recently, I saw a post where a man was complaining that women nowadays were expecting dates to be booked at very fancy venues that you would typically go to for a special occasion. What made me laugh is that the man talking basically said that women are crazy for expecting this on a first date, because they are effectively still strangers in the beginning.

In the world of modern dating, ambitious women often face a unique challenge: the balance between setting high standards and coming off as asking for too much. What this man doesn't know is that there are places in the world, perhaps not where he lives, where this is the bare minimum. I know women in the Middle East who have been sent dozens and dozens of roses to their door before the man has even had a chance to verify whether they are catfish or not, let alone go on a single date with them!

So, I hear you asking...

"OK, so what should be the standard then?"

"Which one is the 'right' standard?"

But here's the truth: Everyone's standards will look different. In order for you to establish your own dating standards, think about framing them around your self-worth. When you remove everyone's expectations of what you *should* have, what is it that really lights you up? The idea of what is realistic or not is your own perception.

I remember being younger and just being happy to be in the presence of the man that asked me out on a date. I gave him all the power without actually asking myself what I personally wanted to experience, and whether this aligned with my self-worth.

When you really go inwards and make this kind of personal inquisition from a place that is rooted in love and not fear, the insights you gain serve as a compass that reflects your authenticity, guiding you towards the partnership you deserve. Now I will tell you, up-leveling your standards is always a bit of work at first because you will inevitably feel like a fraud. And that is totally normal. This is the first time that you are being this raw and honest about what you want, and you will most definitely feel the impostor syndrome creeping in at the beginning.

This chapter is about redefining those standards, building them on a foundation of genuineness and alignment with your values, whilst simultaneously learning how to confidently embody them in the dating world.

DATE YOUR WORTH, NOT YOUR WOUND

WHY STANDARDS MATTER (AND HOW FEAR CAN HIJACK THEM)

It's not uncommon for women to confuse high standards with building emotional fortresses. When you've been hurt, betrayed, or left feeling undervalued, it's natural to want to protect yourself. But if your standards are built on the foundation of fear, in other words the fear of being hurt again, abandoned, or being vulnerable then they'll end up repelling the very love you desire.

Take a moment to consider this: *Are your standards empowering you or isolating you? Are they protecting your heart or are they building a wall around it?*

Let's take a moment to look at the difference between standards and walls.

Standards are proactive. They're based on your values and help you identify what you want to attract in a partner. They say, "I'm worthy of love, and this is what I need to feel safe, respected, and cherished." They are also in alignment with the meaningful life that you have already built for yourself, and the one you want to up-level into and maintain moving forward. Standards are based on the level at which you treat yourself, and act as the very bare minimum for what you choose to experience in this life.

Walls are more reactive. They are specifically designed to keep people out of our lives because they are built out of fear and often stem from unresolved pain. Women often confuse standards and walls because of the *high-value woman movement* that is literally all over the internet. Now, do not get me wrong, I love and adore this movement and I truly wish it was more prominent when I were younger, as it would have saved me a lot of trouble. That being said, however, it is not always done correctly. Walls often cosplay as standards basically saying, "I don't trust myself to choose wisely, so I'll keep everyone out."

The key to resetting your standards is to dismantle the walls built by fear and replace them with boundaries rooted in self-respect. This way, you can still be discerning without compromising your level of vulnerability. Sadly, you cannot date and expect to attract a safe and fulfilling love without being vulnerable. In any way you look at it, love is a gamble each time, but you get to determine how much you bet to ensure that you are betting with trust in yourself, and the possibility of receiving returns that are in line with that.

My Journey to Standards-Based Dating

This concept of resetting my standards isn't just something I teach; it's something I've lived. When you are raised by a single mother, you witness firsthand what it looks like to make do with what you have. I was taught to understand when things were limited, and not to ask for too much because my mother simply was unable to give it to me. My father co-parented with her and paid what he was legally obliged to pay (with the odd gift every now and then), but ultimately, it was my mother raising my brother and I off of her own salary. They were never married, so it was not like she received a hefty alimony every month to provide us with a super comfortable and luxurious lifestyle. We weren't dirt poor; we ate every meal, and sometimes she even surprised us with takeout pizza on Fridays or Saturdays. Despite all of this, it still felt like I could personally do with more. This, by the way, is a perfect example of never being ashamed of your desires. I was a kid and knew that I needed more, *even if I hadn't yet experienced more*. I believe that this means my desire was divinely given, and a forecast of the kind of life I would have, as well as the standards I would set for myself in the future.

Fast forward even a few years into my adolescence, and the same not-asking-for-too-much attitude was still there. I was taught to be grateful for the little I had and although this was a humble way to be, it became an issue once I was in my adulthood. The cognitive dissonance between the modest way of living I had always had, and the larger than life desires that I kept having, started to become harder to ignore. I had pushed myself hard through school and into university, because I was determined to have more than my mother was able to give myself and my brother growing up. I wanted to see the world and experience everything I could. With that curiosity came the realization for me that the scope of what was possible in this life had now expanded tenfold.

When it came to dating specifically, my first healthy adult relationships showed me what it was like when your partner just buys you expensive gifts for no reason, or when he plans an entire romantic weekend away with you. I got to see what it was like not to have to hint 101 times to a man when I needed something, and have him just get the message the first time. I got to experience what it was like when a man who understood the assignment of sitting in his true masculinity knew that opening doors, and letting me sit in my femininity was just a no-brainer.

And now? My standards have upleveled even further because men tell me that they already see me as wife material from our first interactions. They understand that the word "girlfriend" is just the bookmark before marriage — this isn't because I have force fed them this but it is because I have raised my own standard of not just being considered the girlfriend you hang around with for a year or so, with no forward plan. And the men that don't get the wife memo? They freak out and disappear, which is exactly what you want. **Your standards should bring an intensity that men who are ready to meet you where you are will either match or run away from.**

And let me just mention that my standards don't just revolve around the material world. When it comes to respect, men understand that I will not tolerate things like stonewalling or any other type of avoidant attachment or aggressive way of communicating, as I am not prepared to forfeit emotional safety for connection. They understand that I am a monogamous woman who takes loyalty seriously, and therefore will not tolerate infidelity, even if it is just a "one-time thing." They understand that I treat my body like a temple and that I do not drink alcohol, smoke, or take any recreational drugs. They therefore do not try to weaponize their love for me as a reason why I should bypass my own boundaries to "have a good time" or "let my hair down" — that is what yoga is for!

So honestly, my standards look *very* different from what they did when I was younger, when my "standards" were built on fear. I was so afraid of being hurt or undervalued, that I inadvertently created barriers that kept love out entirely. And then there were the other times where I had barely any filter at all. These were the times where literally, all sorts of men were welcomed to come into my life. The latter, when I was very young, used to get me into very questionable situations in which, if I am honest with myself, would not have happened had I loved myself, and learned about how to have truly powerful standards. However, everything happens at the exact divine time it is supposed to happen, and therefore I choose to honor the past me as much as I honor the present and future me.

What has been a clear game changer for me, and now for my clients as I channel my own life experiences into my coaching work, is that I got crystal clear on my non-negotiables and embodied them unapologetically. I stopped entertaining men who weren't ready or willing to meet me at my level. I stopped waiting for someone else to validate my worth and started living it.

I have to talk about my dear friend, Lumiere, who when she reads this will laugh because I believe I am the only one on the planet that calls her this nickname, which is the name of the candlestick character from *Beauty and the Beast*. Being slightly older than me, when we were living in the same city, she was on her soulmate mission before I started to tune into this desire for myself. And I remember clearly that day how she mentioned that she told the man that she eventually ended up marrying, and moving halfway across the world for, that she was not here to mess around and wanted her husband. He had laughed at her, and later on in the conversation she reiterated again that she wasn't playing, and she was looking for a husband.

I really feel like this gave me the confidence to try this out for myself. At first, I thought that this was crazy and borderline too much. But my God, does it work. And it didn't take long for their relationship to blossom, for them to get married, and for them to have their own family. So, you see, ladies...being that kind of assertive only wards off the *wrong* kind of men.

Practical Strategies for Resetting Your Standards

Resetting your standards is an act of self-love, but of course it requires real work. As we mentioned earlier in the chapter, your standards should be a reflection of your deepest values. This is where you get to ask yourself: *What matters most to me in a relationship? Is it emotional intimacy, shared goals, or mutual respect?* You can then start thinking about how you can shape your answers into real-life standards for your dating strategy moving forward.

Checklists are important, but there is a step before a checklist that a lot of high-functioning women miss, and that is first focusing on how you want the relationship to make you feel, not just a checklist of traits you want in the other person. And yes, some of the traits will be based on how you want to feel in a partnership. However, starting with what emotions you hope to experience first is what is going to ensure you are leading from a place of open-heartedness, rather than reeling off everything you desire like a shopping list. Let the feelings you want to experience in your next secure partnership also be a guide to help you build your new set of standards.

Now, a list is wonderful, of course, but it is no good if you are not already what you are asking for. Being in alignment with the relationship you want means already being like-for-like of what you attract. Remember, your energy sets the tone.

DATE YOUR WORTH, NOT YOUR WOUND

If you want a partner who's emotionally available, practice emotional availability yourself. If you want someone who is actively mastering conflict management, you need to be doing the same. And if you value honesty, lead with authenticity.

Setting new standards cannot be done without, of course, the B word...BOUNDARIES. Boundaries are about protecting your energy, not just about keeping people out. Be clear about what you will and won't tolerate, but remain open to connection. A key reminder is that boundaries will only ever offend someone who is not willing to meet them, and somehow benefits from you not having them.

Your standards, especially when you raise them to a higher level than you previously had before, will literally irritate some people so much, that you may have people in your circle feel like they no longer resonate with you. Why is that? Because having these higher standards is not just about applying them to your romantic relationships. Once you see how much it benefits you to value yourself so much more, your energy and the ethos of who you allow to be in your life will permeate into every area of your existence. You will find that you will magnetize better people who elevate you, and those that have benefited from you not speaking your truth will naturally fall away. **THIS IS WHAT WE WANT.**

Within this process, note that it takes time and also, leveling up in any area of your life can mean that you will experience some sort of loneliness. You may encounter internal resistance, because at first it will feel so foreign, as if you are trying to be something you're not. A good reminder for yourself is that you are just becoming someone you have not been before.

My advice is that you stay committed to your values and trust that the right partner will meet you there.

Navigating the Talking Stage with Confidence

Now, let's talk about the infamous "talking stage." Being the busy woman you are, you don't have time to waste on endless back-and-forth messaging. The talking stage might feel safe, but it can also be a trap that keeps you stuck in a cycle of fantasy and inaction. The talking stage in itself, however, isn't the enemy. It's a *necessary* filter!

Think of it as a testing ground where you decide who gets access to your time and energy, and who ultimately doesn't. This is why I don't particularly love the idea of some of these new dating app ideas where you go straight to the physical date, because you risk having to do the filtering in real time ON the date. I personally think it is more efficient to alternatively have screened a match in less than a day, and not wasted your precious time meeting someone who is not in alignment with you.

The real problem? You may be approaching the talking stage from a place of insecurity or impatience. You may stay too long, hoping that the other person will step up. You over-share, over-invest, or let yourself get swept up in fantasies about someone you barely know. The result is that you end up having to deal with emotional exhaustion, frustration, and above all...the nagging feeling that dating is just a waste of time.

This book is designed to help you fall all the way back in love with not only being loved, but the process of finding your ideal partner as well. In order to break free and actually get to the face-to-face dating part of the process, you will need a strategy.

When I hear people say dating is a numbers game, I know for a fact they do not have a good dating strategy. Dating is definitely not a numbers game; it's both a dance and a game of chess. Having firm, new, elevated standards is going to help you put together a framework for the talking stage that will reveal true intentions and compatibility way before you ever invest your time and energy in a potential love interest.

You need to set a timeline every time you are involved with a new man you would like to explore a connection with. **The new version of you needs to get attuned to the fact that access to you, for the men who are not in alignment with what you are looking for, is limited and temporary.**

I meet so many women who complain about having what everyone nowadays are calling "pen pals." Their phones are FILLED with dozens of men who just continuously ask them the same surface-level questions for weeks and sometimes months on end about how their day is going or whether or not they have eaten. All of us only have a certain amount of energy per day. If your energy is being invested into conversations with these men who have been poorly vetted in the hope that one of them will be the one that sweeps you off your feet, you are working hard and not smart. By making this a new part of your strategy, you will automatically eliminate the dating fatigue that so many women complain about.

One other key tip: The talking stage is not about divulging your entire life story. Really and truly ladies, this should be treated like the trailer to the movie — the movie being a full-blown relationship with you. Even if he replies with reams of text, you need to keep your responses succinct and to the point. This is part of the psychology of creating intrigue because, naturally if you're getting along, he will want more of you. By keeping your responses laser focused, you train your love interest that if he wants more of you, it comes at a cost. This cost is his investment into building something real with you i.e., moving the relationship forward by asking you out on dates, calling you, messaging you, etc.

CHAPTER 10

FEMININE ENERGY MEETS AMBITION

The balance between embracing feminine energy and maintaining independence can often feel like walking a tightrope. Society encourages you to be ambitious, driven, and self-sufficient — all of which are undeniably important. However, in your pursuit of professional success and financial security, you're often conditioned to suppress the softer, more intuitive aspects of yourself. That being said, feminine energy isn't about weakness or relinquishing independence; it's about creating flow and harmony in every aspect of your life, from love to career.

In this chapter, we explore the power of integrating feminine energy with masculine drive, not as opposing forces, but as complementary strengths that empower you to thrive in both your personal and professional life. We'll also look at how embracing this integration can unlock not only your heart, but also your potential for abundance in every area of life.

UNDERSTANDING FEMININE ENERGY AND AMBITION

Feminine energy isn't about traditional gender roles or becoming passive; it's about embracing qualities like intuition and your innate creativity. These traits are often diminished in the face of a more "masculine" approach to life, which focuses on getting things done through external achievement. Within feminine energy, however, are crucial elements for cultivating fulfilling relationships and manifesting abundance.

Ambition, on the other hand, is deeply rooted in masculine energy: the drive to reach a goal, solve problems, etc. There's a word of warning that comes with a woman being fueled primarily by masculine energy. When ambition dominates without balance, it can lead to burnout, chronic emotional detachment, and even difficulties in love. The secret lies in integrating the two energies to create a dynamic and fulfilling existence.

For ambitious women like yourself, this doesn't mean abandoning your desire to be known for your talents; it means learning to flow between both energies seamlessly.

The Power of Integration: A Client's Journey

One of my clients, whom I'll call, Marina, came to me feeling stuck in every area of her life. On the surface, she was the epitome of success: A high-ranking corporate executive with a six-figure salary and a long list of professional accomplishments. Despite all of this polished exterior though, Marina's life felt stagnant.

She felt disconnected from her career and increasingly exhausted by her workload. When it came to her dating life, it felt like an insurmountable challenge. During one of our sessions, she confessed that she didn't know how to actually let someone else be in control if it wasn't regarding her career. Unless it had a professional outcome, she really didn't understand how or why she needed to learn to surrender and let someone in.

Marina's story is one many ambitious women can relate to. She had been operating almost entirely from masculine energy for years, and while this approach had brought her professional success, it was leaving her drained and unfulfilled when it came to dating. When we discussed her past relationships there was a clear pattern. She was either made to feel powerless, or she was in a dynamic with a man she overpowered. She had no experience of having been in a relationship where there was a balanced, masculine-feminine polarity. This is why the first step in our work together was helping Marina reconnect with her feminine energy, and to do so without sacrificing her ambition.

One of Marina's breakthroughs came when she started to see the connection between her heart and her bank account. She realized that her resistance to receiving help or support in relationships was mirrored in her financial life. Marina had grown up in a household where she frequently heard that money didn't grow on trees. It was therefore embedded into her psyche that once she was an adult, she could not at any point take her foot off the gas, because it would mean losing control and inviting struggle into her life. She came from a much humbler background than the life she'd built for herself, so backtracking to anything less was simply not an option.

Once this was clear as day for her in terms of where this need for control truly stemmed from, it wasn't long before she applied it to her dating life. She stopped leading every conversation, and allowed space for her dates to step into their masculine energy. This didn't mean playing games or pretending to be someone she wasn't; it meant showing up in her full authenticity, while remaining open to receiving effort and care from others. She started to feel lighter and a whole lot more connected to her emotions — something that she felt she had to shut off on a daily basis working in a male-dominated industry.

Today, Marina is thriving in every sense of the word. She's thriving in her career and thriving in motherhood. She is with a man who cherishes her independence while celebrating her softness. "I never knew I could have both," she told me recently. "I thought I had to choose between being successful and being loved. But now I see that these two things can go hand in hand."

This is a powerful reminder that feminine energy is not a threat to ambition because it is, in fact, the key to amplifying it. When you embrace both energies, you create a life that's not only successful, but deeply fulfilling because you are embracing the natural disposition of being in your feminine flow.

Embracing Feminine Energy Without Sacrificing Independence

So how do you begin integrating feminine energy into your life without compromising your independence? The first step is learning how to receive God's / the Universe's gifts — tangible and intangible. This means not only accepting physical gifts, but also being open to receiving miracles, accepting help, taking compliments (without forcefully giving one back to the other person like you owe them something), etc. The art of receiving is really about allowing yourself to receive without guilt or justification.

I will never forget when I was very sick in hospital with a dangerous fever, and all I wanted was for someone to magically make it all go away so I could sleep in peace without pain and feeling like my entire body was on fire. I had a strange moment during my time there — this moment still gives me shivers to this day.

I had a series of nurses who could have been a lot more helpful than they were until after a brief walk around the hospital, I came back to my room, and I could instantly feel the shift in energy. There was a nurse there who was busy making the room more comfortable as if I were a daughter of hers. So much care and thoughtfulness. She had managed to borrow a fan from God only knows where to help me bring my fever down, in the hopes that it would mean I could go home to my own bed. She had changed my bed sheets, laid out a new gown, and she had taken out all of the rubbish in the room. When she welcomed me into the room we had the most effortless conversation. I was very suspicious of her if I'm honest with you, and I thought, "What is this woman actually up to?!"

I told her how I managed to go from thinking I had a stomach bug to being so sick, and having to stay multiple nights in the hospital — she was so attentive to every detail of my story. Anyway, fast forward to the middle of the night...this same nurse woke me up and told me she was breaking me out of my room, and moving me to a much nicer ward where there was AC AND a TV! I was half asleep when she said this, and I was so confused, wondering if this was even real. She assured me that she would get all of my belongings, and all that I had to do was lay back and be wheeled around.

I will never forget that soul-chilling sentence she whispered to me:

"Rachel...accept this. It gets to be easy for you now."

Even writing that sends chills down my spine, because it was like she channeled that message from another realm. The very next day I asked if I would have her as a nurse again and asked for her using her name. I say this with no ounce of a lie...the nursing team on duty that day told me that a nurse under that name didn't work for the hospital.

Sometimes moments like this make you realize that regardless of where you are in life, even if it seems like you are in your lowest of lowest moments, you are always being watched. Your highest calling will grab you by the wrist and force you down a better path no matter what.

During my hospital stay, which spanned weeks on end with no real idea of when I could go home, I had no choice but to do what I teach all of my clients — fall into deep surrender. That is really the essence of feminine energy.

I had spent most of my life thinking that full surrender into this energy would make me weak and also susceptible to some kind of dark force, but I was so wrong. It was when I leaned in to this power when my health finally started improving in the hospital. I eventually accepted where I was at that moment, instead of trying to manipulate the situation from a place of forcing. I just admitted that it was OK that I was where I was. It felt different because this mindset shift came from a powerful place of knowing that everything would be OK if I just stayed connected to God/ angels/ Source, and receive all of the healing that these trained professionals had for me.

So you see in two completely different aspects just how powerful feminine energy is, and why it is so vital that more women on the planet fiercely tap into it as if their life depends on it...because it does. Ultimately, trust in yourself, trust in others, and trust in the process.

Remember that control is not the same as security. True security comes from knowing you are supported, both by yourself and the spiritual world. And may I add...you are created by the most powerful force that exists. *Of course, it wants you to do well. Of course, it wants you to be at peace and love from a secure and healthy place.*

The whole point of this healing journey, as you may be starting to realize, is not just to get a man, a diamond ring and maybe a baby or two. We are all here for a much bigger mission and purpose. Your mission is going to look nothing like mine, and nothing like the person's next to you, etc. This is why each of our existences is so precious, because we were all uniquely brought into this life to complete our own personal assignment. This doesn't mean abandoning structure, but it does mean allowing flexibility and intuition to guide you, especially in relationships.

You can start doing this first by no longer suppressing feelings to maintain a "strong" exterior and honoring your emotions as valuable insights into your needs and desires. Yes, even those desires that deep down you may not feel like you are 100% worthy of having yet. Feminine energy isn't about doing it all daintily and perfectly. It is about being the rawest you can be with yourself, and consistently challenging why you think the thoughts you think. Remember that ambition, regardless of what that ambition is about, whether it is to do with relationships or finances, requires action and forward movement. Growth, however, also happens in stillness. Give yourself permission to rest and reflect as often as possible because this is where the intuitive magic comes to life.

When feminine energy is integrated with ambition, it becomes the key to creating a life where love and success coexist harmoniously. You don't have to choose between your independence and your desire for connection. You can have both, and you deserve both.

THE FORGOTTEN SIDE OF FEMININE ENERGY: APPRECIATION AND RECIPROCITY

There's something we don't talk about enough when it comes to embodying feminine energy, and it's just as vital as learning to receive.

Yes, being in your feminine energy means allowing yourself to be pursued and provided for. It also means softening into your receptive energy, letting a man lead, and not needing to control or compete. But here's the truth that many people skip over: this dynamic only works when you recognize the *part you play* in maintaining that polarity.

To put it plainly, nothing in life is ever truly free.

DATE YOUR WORTH, NOT YOUR WOUND

That's not to say love should feel transactional or conditional, but all healthy relationships operate within an energetic exchange. Giving and receiving are two halves of the same heartbeat. Without reciprocity, not in material form, but in energy, what you have isn't a relationship; it's one person slowly draining the other person.

We are all human. We all want to feel valued. And whether we admit it or not, everyone likes to receive something in return. That's not greed — that's biology, psychology, and emotional balance working hand in hand.

So yes, be the woman who lets her man lead and receives with grace, but also be the woman who *sees* him and notices his effort. Be the woman who appreciates his consistency and reflects his love back to him in a way that fuels the connection. This doesn't mean over-functioning or mothering your partner — not at all. It means that while he's providing, protecting, and leading, you're meeting him with softness and genuine gratitude. That's feminine power in action.

Let me be clear: appreciation doesn't mean matching his effort tit-for-tat. **Masculine energy thrives on *direction*:** he gives, leads, builds, and protects because that's what makes him feel purposeful. **Feminine energy thrives on *recognition*:** by seeing, admiring, and acknowledging that effort, you breathe life back into his purpose.

So no, you don't have to compete with his giving. But every now and then, it's powerful to make a gesture that says, "I see you."

It can be something as simple as:

- Picking up his favorite coffee when you meet.

- Treating him to a spontaneous meal — not because you have to, but because you *want* to.

- Buying tickets to something he's always talked about doing.

- Leaving a note in his car or a message that reminds him of how much you appreciate his presence.

It's not about the money. It's about the *energy* behind it. When you give from an authentic place, you reinforce the masculine in him. You remind him that he's doing a good job. You tell him, "I see how much you give, and it doesn't go unnoticed."

Men respond incredibly well to this. In fact, it's one of the biggest secrets in male psychology — positive reinforcement. When a man feels respected, appreciated, and *seen*, it amplifies his desire to provide and protect. He's naturally wired to move toward what feels good and what feels rewarding. So when your energy becomes that safe space, when you celebrate his effort instead of taking it for granted, you don't have to *ask* for more. He just does more.

Balancing Giving and Receiving

Here's where a lot of women get confused. They hear "don't chase, don't overgive," which is 100% true, but they take it to mean "don't give anything at all." That's when things start to feel one-sided and robotic. Remember that just as women don't want to feel used, men don't want to feel taken for granted.

DATE YOUR WORTH, NOT YOUR WOUND

When the giving only flows one way, resentment eventually follows, even in the most generous man. The polarity that once created attraction begins to weaken because appreciation is missing. Being in your feminine power doesn't mean being passive or entitled. It means being intuitive, emotionally intelligent, and attuned enough to know when to lean in and when to lean back.

Your intuition is your greatest tool here. It tells you *when* to step forward and offer something nurturing, and when to simply receive and allow. It keeps you in balance — not performing, not withholding — but co-creating. When you tune in to your intuition, it will tell you what gesture fits the moment. It might whisper, "He's had a long week, surprise him with something small." Or it might say, "He's showing up beautifully, keep letting him lead."

Feminine energy isn't formulaic; it's fluid. It's not about ticking boxes, it's about *feeling* into what the relationship needs to stay alive and thriving without forcing anything.

Be the woman who knows that true partnership isn't about who gives more, it's about both people giving differently, but equally meaningfully. That's the balance that keeps love alive and that's the magic that keeps polarity burning.

CHAPTER 11

MASTERING THE DATING FUNNEL

Now we can get on to the practical strategy part of this whole thing. If you're reading this book, chances are you've never left your career, business, or financial life to chance. You've taken radical responsibility for your success at every step of the way; however, when it comes to your dating life, *how intentional have you truly been*? I know so many women who even when they take very long breaks between dating and focusing on themselves, they return to the dating game with just as much frustration as they had before.

Here's the reality though: Love is not a passive game. Just like your career or business, it requires strategy as well as daily and intentional action. Heavy on the DAILY. And heavy on the INTENTIONAL. This is what I call **Mastering the Dating Funnel**. This is a framework for dating with purpose and precision whilst keeping your feminine energy intact.

In this chapter, we're going to dismantle the idea that love is some random thing. It is not a mystery, and it is not something you, for some reason, do not have the intelligence to understand and make work for you, in the way you desire it to. I'll show you how to bring structure and intentionality to your dating life without turning it into another exhausting task. When done right, calling in husband material men happens almost on autopilot and dare I say it...the whole process actually becomes *fun*.

WHY YOU NEED A DATING FUNNEL

You wouldn't leave your business lead generation strategy or your next career move up to luck, so why would you do this in your love life? This is why, just like a funnel to attract clients or having a strong network for career growth are both necessary in business and the corporate world, a dating funnel is required for attracting the right kind of romantic partners. But what is a funnel? A funnel is simply a framework that moves people from "curious stranger" to "deep connection," whilst filtering out those who aren't aligned and drawing in those who actually are.

When applied to dating, your funnel helps you:

Identify Quality Prospects Quickly and Filter Out Time-Wasters/Emotionally Unavailable Men

This means that you only end up on dates, and investing your energy into men who could potentially be long-term partner material based on your early interactions. Now, I will say this really loudly to you, it does not mean you are immune to men who will want to waste your time. You have to remember that you are like a seven-figure-paying job with an annual bonus, massive pension, and car allowance in a metropolitan city with a tropical climate. Basically, who *isn't* going to apply for that job?! Everyone is going to try and get it even though they know, for damn sure, they are not even remotely qualified to even get to the interview stage.

Dating is like the national lottery where a lot of people understand that if they don't play, they can't be in with a chance of winning. This therefore means they lose *nothing* by submitting their application! I am pointing this out because men who are not what you are looking for will still be drawn to you, and it is not a sign that you are doing something wrong. **It is the reality of being a magnetic woman.**

By learning how to discern between who moves on to the next stage in the dating process with you, i.e. meeting properly for a date, this helps to minimize how long you spend on men who are masquerading as prince charming. You can then save both your energy and your heart for someone who is more likely to be a long term, fulfilling match. This is why again, I do not buy into the propaganda that dating is a numbers game. You should ideally be going on relatively few first dates if you are doing this correctly, specifically because it is not a numbers game. It is a process where you gate-keep your energy in a way that is protective of your peace, and is a reflection of the deep desire you want for quality and lasting partnership.

Move From Initial Conversation to First Date Efficiently

This is so important because I am sure you have experienced the chronic pen-pal dynamic where you are just talking endlessly with a man for weeks or months on end, and it literally goes nowhere. They normally aren't "bad" people, but the needle doesn't get moved even when it is clear that you were both interested in the beginning and perhaps initially, you both expressed wanting very similar things.

When you have the right structure in place for your own bespoke dating funnel, you will never again be caught in this stalemate because the standards will be so different from the ones you are operating in now. What is missing from your strategy currently are parameters for, what is my favorite word...ACCESS. Speaking to you is privileged access and with that privilege should come limitations and a cease of that access if things are not moving along. It is not a case of being unkind because remember this, every day you give to someone who just continues to ask you surface level questions week after week with no actual plan, is another day where you are kept from meeting your potential husband. Why? Because you only have so much emotional bandwidth in a day. So if you are spending part of your daily energetic allowance on someone who isn't moving the needle, then no wonder you feel burned out. This is not going to give you the ROI you are looking for, so why entertain any prolonged involvement with someone like this?

Having said that, it is not just about having parameters, but also knowing what needs to be done in the actual conversation part, whether this be a voice call, video call, or just text/WhatsApp messages. Your chats should feel natural, of course, but they also need to be intentional and strategic. Asking what their favorite color is can be cute, but I want you to think about the fact that this is a screening process. So, if their favorite color is green, that doesn't give you the information you need in order to determine whether or not, for example, this person has a history of being chronically non-committal, which is more important.

And even more importantly, the conversation absolutely needs to be geared towards a face-to-face date...**without you leading**. When you get this right, you will be able to sprinkle enough feminine energy to make it clear that this is what you're available for without actually directly suggesting, and planning the whole thing. Remember, you are not here to do the man's job for him — if you want that masculine-feminine polarity, *you must let him be the one who believes it was his idea to ask you out on a date.* This is imperative.

Foster Meaningful Connections Whilst Honoring Your Energy

Having your own dating funnel is going to ensure things are kept respectful and drastically improve your dating experience. This really is a product of you being zeroed in on what it is that you are looking for and what it is that you are willing to tolerate. Without a dating funnel, many women fall into one of two traps:

The "Whatever Happens, Happens" Trap: This is passive, reactive dating with no clear vision or boundaries.

The "Hustle & Grind" Trap: This involves you over-functioning, chasing, and burning out in the dating process.

The spoiler is that neither of these methods will get you the deep, committed love you want because they both prevent you from fostering the genuine, grounded self-worth and vulnerability required.

Optimizing your dating funnel is a key part of the *Attract Your Equal* formula (my signature program that I talk about more later in the book); however, I have broken it down briefly below so that you can start implementing it to an extent in your own lives as of today:

YOUR DATING FUNNEL BLUEPRINT

Here's a simplified version of how your dating funnel should flow:

1. **Visibility & Connection** (Initial Attraction)

2. **Pre-Qualification & Alignment/Intent Check** (Messaging & Early Conversations)

3. **First Initial Dates & Emotional Screening** (Moving Offline)

4. **Exclusive Dating & Deep Connection** (Commitment Stage)

Each phase requires deep intention and your unwavering, clear standards to come together as part of your strategic action. An example of this is my client, who had never been in a committed relationship in her entire adult life and knew she didn't want to continue that way any longer (we will call her, Celine). She is one of those clients who are impossible to forget because her personality was just so infectious that you just wanted to carry on talking to her for ages. This is someone who, as part of the type of work she was involved in, was in a different country more often than people can even fathom. Even when things were calmer for her during her slower seasons, she seemed to repeatedly find herself with a full roster of very good-looking men who were practically just fans of her. One time she showed me her Instagram DMs, and I saw that she was flooded with messages daily. But even when she engaged with men who she wouldn't mind going on a date with, the conversations just stayed surface level.

It wasn't until we really got to the bottom of this that things started to actually happen for her. It was clear that she was able to attract men with her eyes closed; that was a given. What was wonderful was being there to witness Celine realize that her nonchalant attitude towards love when she so deeply was searching for someone she could build a life with, was just not really getting her what she wanted. She realized that on some level, she was settling for the idea that love perhaps was never going to be a reality for her, and so she happily entertained the fan base without ever really looking into why none of these connections turned into partnerships.

Celine today is nothing like she was back then. Yes, being what a lot of people would deem to be unfairly beautiful on top of her rock star personality, she still has her DMs full of roaring male fans. When it comes to who she is dating now, however, she is currently sifting through men with real grounded intention and making it clear from the very beginning what she is available for. She admitted to me that it felt very strange doing so in the beginning, as her personality is so happy-go-lucky, but that she was grateful for learning these strategies. She confessed that they have helped her feel like she is actually getting closer to finding her man, and also that it is possible because she has a real game plan that she didn't have in place before.

Your own dating life deserves the same strategy, structure, and care you give to every other area of your success. Notice how Celine on paper sounds like a woman who had it all going for her. I am sure you can not only just identify with her in this respect, but you can also say the same about the single women in your close circle of friends. I use Celine as an example because I want to show you that it is simply not enough to just be a wonder woman alone. The higher powers that be are not just going to drop a perfect relationship in your lap without your deliberate involvement, *the right way*.

I also share her story because I know how many of us were raised, especially by our mothers, grandmothers, and aunts to believe that beauty is both a blessing **and** a kind of silent curse. We were subtly taught that being too beautiful might actually make love harder to find. The message transmitted to us was that others might assume we already have everything we need so we're overlooked, that our desirability somehow disqualifies us from being treated seriously, or fairly.

Let's squash that myth once and for all. You are not jinxed and there is **nothing wrong** with being beautiful and desired. It is not something you need to tone down or apologize for. You just need to discern between who gets to audition to be a part of your life, and who stays at the door. And above all, you need to learn how to do this with enough ease that you do not get burned out in the process.

CHAPTER 12

ATTRACTING YOUR EQUAL

You've heard it said before: "You attract what you are." And while it sounds poetic, for the kind of woman you are, this truth often hits a *little too hard*. When your standards are high, your dreams are big, and your energy is powerful, you start to notice how rare it is to meet someone who truly feels like an equal and can match you emotionally, intellectually, and energetically.

But here's the real challenge: Many women think they're attracting the wrong men because of a lack of options. In reality, it's often because they're not yet fully aligned with the version of themselves who is ready to receive their equal. And also...notice I said rare, *not impossible*. **No, ladies, these men are not going to magically appear every day, but that isn't the point.** Step one of attracting your equal is throwing tired timelines out of the window. I know that can feel so counter-intuitive because you are the master planner who has full control of every piece of her life. *I get it.*

This chapter is about doing the work to become the woman who naturally attracts and receives a partner on her level. *You don't have to settle for less in order to settle down.* You can have the love you desire without sacrificing your standards or softening your ambition. Attracting your equal is about more than finding a man who earns a similar income or has a similar lifestyle. It's about emotional maturity, relationship readiness, values alignment, and energetic compatibility.

Trust me, there are plenty of well-off men who are emotionally bankrupt, and unlike certain "coaches" out there, my advice is not that you pimp yourself out to these men at all costs even if it means abandoning yourself just so you can live the "soft life." Absolutely not. Those "coaches" and influencers make me laugh, because yes, whilst they add so much entertainment value, it is actually so unhealthy teaching women to shut off their emotions so that they can financially benefit from a man they feel nothing for.

You will know you have met someone you can consider your equal when you have consistent evidence over time that they:

- Respect your ambition without feeling threatened by it.

- Match your emotional intelligence and capacity for intimacy.

- Show up with integrity and demonstrate that they have the ability to build something meaningful with you.

- Share a similar vision for partnership and the future you are co-creating together.

This is definitely not about finding a man to "complete" you; it's about connecting with someone who complements you, grows with you, and builds alongside you.

There is a warning that comes with this. Discerning whether you are being met in this kind of way in a relationship sometimes means that, along the journey, you will meet matches who are simply mirroring back to you who you are and what you desire. These are the kinds of men who are trained chameleons and really struggle with building their own authentic identity. When they see your glowing empathetic persona, they copy yours in the hopes that you won't notice that theirs is in fact counterfeit. The only defense against this is truly taking your time to get to know a person. Someone who is wearing a mask can only do so for so long before the cracks start to show, and they reveal the fact that they were in cosplay as your soulmate. The reality is that they are just not capable of providing the depth of connection that you seek.

The Inner Work Behind Attracting Your Equal

But let's not focus on them — let's focus on what is actually within your control, and that is your inner work. The quality of your love life is a direct reflection of the relationship you have with yourself. If you're still entertaining situationships, emotionally unavailable partners, or men who make you question your worth, it's not because good men don't exist. It's because there's still a part of you that accepts that kind of love and feeds into that reality.

The neural pathways in our brains are like elastic bands or chewing gum — super malleable, and they can take ANY shape we want. Therefore, whatever you have programmed in your mind as the "truth" can be undone and rewired to reflect a new reality. This is true even if you have been thinking certain beliefs your whole life. Everything can be rearranged and redesigned to fit your new reality, **should you choose to commit to doing this.** So, if you are ready, here's what attracting your equal requires you to do:

1. **Do the Inner Healing:** We have touched on core wounds and attachment styles already in the book so that is your cue again to note this down as something that is absolutely fundamental. Meaning no matter how boring and lonely the healing journey is (because it is both of those things), if you want to see different results, you need to stick to the plan and not follow your mood. This is the only way to truly be able to heal your inner child, and be confident that as a result of your hard work, your dating experience is going to be vastly different.

2. **Embody Your Worth:** We have also discussed standards and over-functioning when it comes to love. Embodying your worth means already trying on these new mantras and tactics as if you are already the woman you are trying to become. If you struggle with doing this without an example, I know just the thing that will help. On social media, find yourself three role models that embody

the kind of confidence and powerful femininity that you want to take on from now. Make notes about how they speak or present themselves and then — don't just copy them...but adapt these things to your own style. *Make it yours.* With some trial and error, you will develop your own unique style, which will form part of the irresistible dating strategy you are building that is bespoke to you and your desires.

3. **Lead with Authenticity**: This is so important when you are out in the dating world as a strategy that will ward off men with narcissistic behavior traits. Authenticity...yes, that's the start of it, but the gift that showing up authentically gives you is that you radiate a self-sufficient confidence. Do this right and anyone coming to manipulate you, will find that you will call them out on their BS quickly. Real recognizes real, but it also recognizes fake. Men that you call out on their BS as being fake will turn around and tell you that you are "hard work." That's when you know you are *really* doing a good job.

4. **Be Available for What You Want**: This is a hard one to drop but here goes...ladies, stop entertaining what doesn't align with your vision. I want you to think of your energy as a compass. Where it is directed is what you are trying to manifest more of. With that being said, even though I understand and appreciate that we all have needs, I am strongly against casual sexual arrangements. Here's why: As much as you think you can trick your brain into being stoic, and just being in it for the physical, even if you manage to achieve this facade in the moment, going against what you truly desire is a

micro act of self-betrayal. You don't want the guy who any woman can sleep with. You know the type of man I mean. The type of man where no matter what time of year, you know when you call him, he is ready to pull up outside wherever you are. You don't want what he is offering. You are stronger than that. You are worth more than that. **And trust me, from a very sensual woman like myself, sex is great, but without that soulmate connection...it is just naked exercise.** Save your spirit and your wonderful body for a relationship where that man has earned that kind of treasure and, above all, you are both on the same page as to where the relationship is going.

My recommendation to clients is to think of those moments of weakness like craving fast food right before your holiday, and you have spent months working out in preparation for it. It is not going to be worth breaking your diet because, if you just wait another extra 10 to 20 minutes, the mind will have a new trail of thought to follow, and you will no longer want to ruin your hard work for a short-term pleasure. It is exactly the same when it comes to holding out sexually for someone who you are genuinely getting to know, and would like to pursue a serious relationship with.

Allow thoughts about reaching out to your casual flings/sneaky links to come and go. You do not have to assign any meaning to them — having them does not mean that you are doing anything wrong; it just means you are human. Regularly not allowing them to dictate your next action is the real power move, and this will take practice...but you *will* get there.

DATE YOUR WORTH, NOT YOUR WOUND

Why Accomplished Women Struggle to Attract Their Equal

When you're stuck in the hyper-masculine, 24/7 on the go, controlling, fixing mode, you're more likely to attract men who want to be "taken care of," or who resent your success. Alternatively, and as we have discussed earlier, you may unconsciously chase emotionally unavailable partners because it feels familiar or "safe." Why do I say this?

Well, as we have realized together in this book, strong women like yourself are forged out of fire. You didn't have it all the way easy in life — I mean nobody does, but you know that you are a special breed. Becoming the force you are didn't come out of choice. It was survival. So while attracting someone who matches or exceeds your level is essential, protecting the life you've built, against all odds, is non-negotiable. In other words, your mental health is not for sale. Attracting your equal requires you to lean into your feminine energy — yes — but *without sacrificing your inner fire.*

An example of that is a wonderful client of mine that we will call Victoria. Due to her profession, she is ridiculously well educated. In fact, I believe she must have spent more than a third of her life in education, in order to become qualified in what she does now. And yet, when we first started working together, we noticed something that she had carried from her childhood into her adult relationships.

This was that because she earned a high salary and was so educated, this resulted in her facing situations where she was made to feel like just by existing, she was already "too much" and "too boastful." This, of course, was not the case, and she was simply surrounded by people who saw her success as a threat. This is not because it actually was, of course. It was because, in theory, she shouldn't be doing as good as she was in life considering how she was raised. It was like unintentionally holding a mirror up to these people in her world, who had a closet full of unrealized dreams and untapped potential. Instead of her success acting as a source of inspiration for them, they found it deeply threatening and then weaponized their own inner-shame against her.

This meant that at an early stage, Victoria had learned that being proud of her accomplishments, or even bringing them up was a trigger for conflict. As you can imagine, this was a magnet for insecure men who made her feel like she had to dim her shine in order to keep the peace. It also meant that she subconsciously chose men who weren't on the same level as her — and of course not. It wasn't what she was used to. She was used to dating lower than her level.

Now, when I say this, I do not mean that the men she chose were any less worthy as human beings because of their level of success. What I mean is in terms of being able to pour equally into a healthy, secure, mutually beneficial relationship, these men were never able to meet her where she was at.

Despite this, she stayed in cycles with these men because it was familiar and predictable. She had perfected this act from a young age, and therefore being with someone she could consider her equal was, quite frankly, a terrifying thought. It was unknown territory that she wasn't prepared to try to venture into, because the effects of her childhood trauma were still playing out.

She had no trouble attracting men — I have to say for some reason, I get the most magnetic women wanting to work with me! It is not just about physical beauty; I get the most radiant women who have so much inner magic, that it excites me when they reach a part of their journey where they are ready to switch things up when it comes to relationships. Victoria was no different.

Through our work together in my signature program, *Attract Your Equal,* she is now in a loving relationship with someone who is finally in alignment with everything she offers, and boy, does it show!

In our recent catch-up call, she told me how she is so enamored with her new man, who she locked down in just a matter of months. He is more on the creative side in terms of profession, but nonetheless just as hungry for success as she is. It was so beautiful to watch her glow as she expressed finally being cheered on, and supported by her partner. She told me how much she particularly *loved* not having to hide the fact she received promotions, or had been asked to be a speaker at events. One thing she said that still makes me quite emotional is this: "All of this work...it's actually paid off."

Even though my clients on this program walk away completely transformed and swear by the framework, I always emphasize that the framework is only one part. Their decision to change their lives and stay devoted to the future they want to create for themselves is what truly brings those incredible results.

So, what about you? If you could do the same, what would you be willing to do to also attract a man who you can see yourself building a life with?

He Doesn't Need Your LinkedIn Bio

It may feel counter-intuitive, but I want you to know that you don't have to "prove" your worth. What I mean by this is that it is not required for a successful woman to showcase her resume on dates or even on dating profiles.

I have spoken to highly successful men who have literally shown me profiles that they would reject, even when the woman is age appropriate for them and looks like a complete catch due to this very reason.

One profile I remember being shown basically said the words PhD and TEDx speaker at the very top of the bio. The profile then proceeded to list every single thing she *wasn't* looking for, followed by the hook at the end: "Swipe right if you're interested." Ladies, let me give you a tip. How I speak to men about what I do is not the way I speak to women about what I do. Why? Because as of right now (who knows if this will change in the future), men are not my target audience...women are. And therefore, the wording is different even if I am talking about the same thing. I am suggesting the same advice when you are out on the market looking for a serious relationship with a man.

There's a fine balance I teach all my clients which is how to stand confidently in their achievements, without feeling the need to push every success in a man's face from day one. Think about it. Many women who aren't reading this book, but may hear me say this, might ask, *"But isn't that shrinking?"* No, it isn't — it's emotional intelligence.

Even in a room full of women, if someone constantly lists everything they've accomplished, would you feel drawn to them? Or would you instinctively sense that they're trying to prove something? Leading with your accolades blocks genuine connection from forming right from the start.

When women do this, it's often less about confidence and more about protection. Whether they realize it or not, it is an attempt to appear impenetrable, like an entire continent standing alone. And while self-assurance is a beautiful thing, the truth is, they're preaching to the wrong audience!

The secret to attracting your equal is not about being prettier, smarter, having more money, etc. It is about how far you are really prepared to go to peel back the layers of yourself, and show up completely "naked." It is about being honest about how badly you want to experience love differently, so that you attract someone who is just as ready as you are to build an entirely new chapter of life together.

If you're ready to take this work deeper, I invite you to watch my training: *Becoming the Woman Who Attracts Her Equal.*

BONUS TRAINING

BECOMING THE WOMAN WHO ATTRACTS HER EQUAL

In this training, I show you how to embody the energy and mindset of a woman who attracts love that truly matches her. You'll learn how to integrate your feminine and masculine energies, date from alignment, and become magnetic to emotionally secure, high-quality partners who meet you where you are.

You'll discover:

- How to shift from chasing or over-performing in love to *receiving* and allowing partnership to meet you with ease.

- The energetic and behavioral traits of women who naturally attract emotionally available men and keep them.

- How to show up as your authentic, high-value self in dating and relationships without playing games or compromising your standards.

HOW TO ACCESS YOUR BONUS TRAINING

1. **Go to** https://www.rachelroseonline.com/ .

2. **Select "Video Trainings."**

3. **Select the relevant training for this chapter and use code "YOUAREWORTHY" at checkout for free access.**

CHAPTER 13

THE ART OF COMMITMENT

For many ambitious women, commitment isn't just about securing a title — it's about feeling safe and prioritized. Yet when deeper issues go unaddressed, what often follows is a blend of weak boundaries and fear-based behavior. In an effort to appear "easygoing" or "low maintenance," you end up tolerating mixed signals and emotional ambiguity, hoping that familiarity alone will eventually lead to commitment. If you're at this chapter, you have already read *a lot* so far, so congratulations. It is likely that you're ready to talk about the next step: **turning potential into partnership.**

This is a chapter I have been dying to write because this is where so many women get stuck. You are not brand new to male attention, so you know how to start things, but turning casual conversations into committed relationships feels confusing and sometimes exhausting. And social media certainly doesn't help. More and more people are creating content that reinforces the same narrative: that finding someone emotionally secure and ready to commit is a modern-day pipe dream. This message spreads easily because, on some level, it's comforting to believe that on such a vast planet, you're not the only one wondering why you're still single. But sharing that dissatisfaction online, whether you're the one creating the posts or passively consuming them, doesn't bring you any closer to what you truly want.

The quality of information you consume as a single woman has as much of a direct correlation with your success in dating, as your practical strategy does. If you are consuming reels and posts that perpetuate the fact that finding a committed relationship is so hard, it will never happen for you. I think that is the bluntest sentence I have written in the book so far, but it is absolutely true. You'll either find yourself alone for an extended season of your life, or caught in the dreaded situationship cycle wondering how you ended up in yet another undefined and unfulfilling connection. **But it doesn't have to be that way.**

In this chapter, we're going to walk through the feminine art of nurturing a connection from the first date to exclusivity without manipulation or confusion. Commitment is not about chasing or convincing; it's about setting clear boundaries, communicating your standards, and confidently holding space for the right man to meet you there.

WHY COMMITMENT FEELS HARD (ESPECIALLY FOR SUCCESSFUL WOMEN)

It is not uncommon to have the belief that a man you casually date (i.e. not with intention), will just magically see your value one day, and commit. Women who buy into this way of thinking however, are just scared of the bravery that is involved in being 100% upfront about what they want from the beginning with a man. More often than not, this is because they do not want to look like they *need* a relationship. Can you relate to this?

The truth is, nobody *needs* a relationship. But a huge part of your healing is admitting that you deeply desire it. You love the idea of it and have room in your life for it, but it is an additional bonus to your life — not the foundation of your existence. When you can make that vision real, and it truly feels authentic to you, you create the perfect foundation to start showing up with clarity and confidence in dating. From that place, you can be direct with men about what you're looking for from day one. The unspoken rule of life is simple: if you're vague about your desires, you'll attract vague...because that's exactly what you ordered!

Some of the heartbreak stories you hear come from women who preferred not to look "too needy" and just decided to go with the flow. In fact, some of these women end up in heated arguments with men they've coasted along with for months, eventually exploding out of frustration over the lack of progression in the relationship. In these scenarios, the men involved feel blindsided because they were given little to no indication that a serious relationship is what the women they are dating wanted.

But real, lasting commitment isn't something that just *happens* to certain people. It's the result of intention, self-awareness, and alignment. And if you're still doubting your potential, let me offer you a little perspective. Some of history's most ruthless rulers, serial killers, and thieves *all had spouses*. So clearly, lasting relationships aren't reserved for the "lucky" or the "perfect." Even the most unhinged examples of humanity have managed to find someone willing to commit.

So when you bring that back to yourself: **an extraordinary, hardworking, deeply empathetic, beautiful, funny, intelligent woman like you...** *why wouldn't that be not only possible, but inevitable?*

SETTING THE STAGE FOR COMMITMENT

So to conclude this chapter, if you're tired of undefined relationships, the path to commitment starts with YOU. It doesn't suddenly show up because you secretly hoped the man you're interested in would read your mind. One thing that women need to understand about male psychology is that even the nicest man on Earth will take what they can from a woman for free. Why wouldn't they? It is frankly unfair to fake being open to casual whilst deeply desiring a serious relationship, and not voice this to the person you are dating. Women complain that they are coerced into situationships, but unless you explicitly stated that you wanted something more, you cannot place all of the blame on the man or on whatever higher being you believe in. **Now more than ever, as a high-value woman searching for her soulmate, you need to shout it from the rooftops exactly what you are looking for.**

Even the animals know they need to do this! Have you ever seen an animal in their own habitat who wants a mate just hang around crossing their fingers? Both sexes actually usually get involved, whether it's the females placing themselves in the right environments for eligible males or the males going out of their way to make sure they are in the right place to mate. It is instinctual to position themselves accordingly in order to achieve their desired outcome. It is just us humans that complicate things! Positioning yourself correctly includes asking yourself:

- "Am I clear on what I want and need in a relationship?"

- "Have I communicated those needs openly and without fear?"

- "Am I willing to walk away if my needs aren't met?"

The key is to create an environment where commitment can flourish through clear communication and healthy boundaries. That way, EVERYONE is a winner.

NAVIGATING THE "WHAT ARE WE?" STAGE

Let's talk about that *awkward* moment which is the space between early dating and official commitment. You've been seeing someone for a few months. The chemistry is undeniable, the connection feels real, and yet... the relationship still hasn't been defined. You both sense the topic lingering in the air, but it never feels like the right time to bring it up.

Now, after everything we've discussed in this book about feminine energy, I'm not about to tell you to lead this conversation in a way that pulls you out of your power. Defining a relationship is a delicate process that requires grace and patience. In adulthood, choosing a partner isn't casual; it's an act of *investment*. When you agree to be with someone exclusively, you're essentially saying:

"I'm choosing to pour into you: emotionally, energetically, and financially."

That's why so many of us have become far more discerning post-COVID. We no longer give our time or energy away freely — whether it's to jobs, friendships, or potential partners. Just as professionals now turn down six-figure roles that don't align with their wellbeing, modern women are learning not to accept relationships that compromise their peace.

You no longer need to fear this part of the dating process. I want to help you *navigate this stage like an absolute boss*, so that you are fully anchored in your feminine energy. First, let's reframe this: your title *is* coming. Don't spiral into the frantic energy of overthinking when or how it will happen. As I often remind my clients, the question is never *if* — it's *when*.

My work protects women from staying in this "waiting period" indefinitely. I even have a specific time frame I recommend as the maximum amount of time to wait before walking away and redirecting your energy elsewhere. Once you understand that this phase is temporary, that you'll either move into a formal relationship with the person you're seeing, or be gracefully redirected toward a more aligned partner...the panic begins to dissolve.

Now, let's talk about that 1–3 month period of dating which is the stage of assessing whether this connection truly fits. You may feel tempted to bring up the conversation directly. However, if your goal is to create a relationship with masculine-feminine polarity, I don't recommend initiating that discussion. If you want to attract leadership, you must create the *space* for it to emerge. Allow him to claim you in his timing because it sets the tone for the partnership that follows.

That doesn't mean you sit passively in silence. There will be moments where you exchange intimate, couple-like conversations followed by the silence of "who's going to say it first?" Instead of filling that gap with anxiety, use it to *deepen your energy*. Stay curious and open by asking feminine-based, exploratory questions that reveal values, alignment, and emotional depth without directly bringing up labels.

So, how does a connection naturally build toward commitment? This is where many women misunderstand male psychology. For emotionally healthy men who embody leadership and provision, the decision to commit doesn't happen in the moment, face-to-face. It happens when they experience the *contrast* of your presence versus your absence. When he's with you, he feels peace and expansion. When you leave, he realizes how much your energy elevates his life. That contrast creates emotional depth and drives him to ensure he doesn't lose you. This is the natural progression that leads to commitment.

Sometimes, commitment unfolds naturally without a formal conversation, perhaps through an introduction as "my girlfriend" or "my partner." That counts too. You can always clarify afterward if you need verbal confirmation. Remember: we are not in high school. In many cultures, men express commitment through consistent action rather than direct words. In this instance, if you need clarity, you have every right to ask for it in a calm, grounded way.

One final note: please don't hyperfocus on getting the title. Plenty of men throw around labels easily but real, secure men do not. For them, commitment represents something sacred. Even if they aren't dating multiple people, they know that becoming someone's partner means being accountable and showing up consistently.

Men who are serious about their purpose or careers often won't enter relationships lightly. They want to be *ready* to provide and protect. Allow that process to unfold and let your connection breathe. Give space for conflict, boundary-setting, and real-life moments to surface. These are the tests that reveal whether your relationship is built on fantasy or true foundation, and we know that you both want and deserve the latter.

PART THREE: JOURNAL REFLECTION AND AFFIRMATIONS

Embodiment is when healing becomes visible. It's not just about knowing your worth; it's about *moving* like a woman who does. Every choice you make — how you speak, what you allow, and what you walk away from — is a reflection of your embodied energy.

This section helps you align your behavior with your highest self.

PROMPTS:

1. **Embodied Version of You**
   The most magnetic woman in the room isn't the loudest — she's the most grounded.
   How does the most confident, radiant version of me carry herself in love and life?

2. **Releasing Old Patterns**
   When you rise in self-worth, old habits feel heavy.
   What behaviors or tendencies no longer align with the woman I'm becoming?

3. **Receiving with Ease**
   Many women struggle to receive love.

How can I practice receiving support — emotionally, financially, or romantically — without guilt?

4. **Boundaries and Softness**
   Boundaries aren't walls; they're invitations for respect.
   What boundaries allow me to feel both safe and soft?

5. **Leading from Feminine Power**
   True leadership in love isn't control — it's energetic clarity.
   How can I lead in love through openness, authenticity, and emotional intelligence rather than performance or force?

PART FOUR: EXPANSION

"The woman who trusts her timing feels the fear of what's leaving and what's yet to come, but chooses to surrender anyway." — *Rachel Rose*

CHAPTER 14

THE ABUNDANT YOU: LOVE AND WEALTH IN ALIGNMENT

You've heard the saying, "How you do one thing is how you do everything." This could not be truer than when it comes to the relationship between love and money. Most accomplished women who come to me believe their struggles in love are isolated from their experience with their finances.

In this chapter, we are going to shift the narrative around this completely.

You'll learn how the energy you hold around love is the same energy you hold around money. If you have fear in one area, it will inevitably show up in the other. This is not about manifestation hacks or toxic positivity. This is about real, practical alignment of your inner world and your external world so you can thrive in both your relationships and your financial endeavors.

THE ENERGETIC CONNECTION BETWEEN LOVE AND MONEY

In my opinion, love and money at their core are both about harnessing feminine energy. They're both essentially about **receiving**. The truth is, both love and money mirror your inner belief system: *you can only receive at the level you believe you're worthy of.*

When you carry deep self-trust, you naturally attract relationships and opportunities that match your value. But it takes a special kind of vulnerability to do this — to stay open enough to receive, instead of trying to control or prove. That's the real key to unlocking romantic and financial abundance.

When I was dating men I knew I was settling for, entrepreneurship wasn't even a thought in my mind. Becoming a manager? I could barely imagine it. Back then, I was just grateful to have a job, let alone believe I was capable of leading an entire team or having my own business.

I remember times in the corporate world when my throat would tighten just from sharing a small opinion, convinced my voice didn't matter. That was the same year I met a man who kept me hanging for months. He kept on promising commitment he never intended to give, while sleeping with half the city behind my back.

As we've discussed, your experience in life is directly tied to what you're willing to tolerate. So, take an honest look...are you currently accepting any of the following in your life?

In Love	In Money
Settling for emotionally unavailable partners who give the bare minimum	Undercharging or settling for financial opportunities that undervalue your worth
Avoiding interpersonal boundaries out of fear of losing the connection	Avoiding financial boundaries out of fear of missing out or seeming "selfish"
Ignoring red flags because you see potential	Ignoring financial warning signs because you hope things will "work out"
Staying in relationships that drain you	Staying in jobs or investments that deplete you
Believing you have to struggle to experience real partnership	Believing you have to struggle to be successful

If you recognize yourself in either column, it's a sign that love and money are reflecting the same wound, and both will shift the moment you decide you're no longer available for anything less than what you truly deserve.

As I write this, there are definitely examples of people I know who have spent their entire existence being at war with both areas of their lives. All that has happened is that their resentment has just continued to grow towards anyone who has mastered both.

For these people, they really think that it must just be the luck of the draw, which, by the way, is the laziest conclusion when it comes to anything you want on this planet. Nothing is just luck of the draw. Mainly because even the flashiest of people or the showiest of couples you see have their own struggles. Being "lucky" is just down to perception. Also, side note, even if the same people lost everything tomorrow, it still wouldn't change *your* relationship with love and money. This is why I learned to keep my eyes on my own life.

The moment you are busy worrying about how well other people are progressing towards the goals you want, you leak the very energy you need to turn your own desires into reality. When you operate from scarcity, you subconsciously block both love and money.

In love, scarcity can sound like believing that there's some magical shortage of good men and you missed your chance. It can also look like treating love as if it's an academic qualification you have to study hard and bleed for, just to be worthy of receiving it.

When it comes to money, scarcity thinking shows up in the same way: believing you have to stay within a certain tax bracket, scale your income only inch by inch (if you're "lucky," there's that word again), and that money is inherently hard to earn or keep. And then there's the ultimate scarcity belief, the one that ties love and money together : **You can't possibly have both. If you succeed in one area, you'll have to sacrifice the other.**

How did it feel reading those beliefs to yourself? Do they uplift you? Do they inspire you to find your dream relationship? Do they inspire you to create financial investments and create generational wealth? Of course they don't. ALL of these beliefs create an energetic contraction that repels abundance.

The scary thing I find is that in a lot of societies on our planet, we have normalized this scarcity mindset and use it as a weird way of social bonding. Somehow, talking about having *less* — less love, less money, less abundance — has become what makes you relatable. Because God forbid you're ever seen as someone who's *too* in love or *too* supported by money. It is total BS and propaganda that I am no longer buying into.

One of the biggest things I say to clients or if I am in a masterclass, then I tell my live audience, is this: **if you come anywhere near my work, I hope you are prepared to become a little unpopular — at least with the wrong people, because the mindset you will move into WILL attract your dream tribe.**

Do you really think that, in millionaire circles, there's an unspoken competition about who has the least or how hard money is to come by? Quite the opposite. Those are the rooms where healthy competition thrives, where each person's success inspires the next to rise higher and do more.

And the same applies to love. When you're surrounded by couples who are deeply connected and intentional, you don't hear endless debates about how "love is broken." It doesn't happen because you're amongst a collective that believes in love, partnership, growth, and teamwork — and they're living proof that it works. The truth is simple: when you expand your capacity to receive love, you naturally expand your capacity to receive wealth and vice versa.

I want to pause here for a moment to acknowledge something important. We live in a world that can often feel chaotic and uncertain at times.

As you read this, you're likely aware of the suffering and inequality that exists in other parts of the world, and maybe even in your own community. That awareness matters because it's what makes you human. But I also want to gently remind you that honoring your blessings doesn't mean ignoring anyone else's pain. You don't have to dim your joy to prove your empathy.

Both realities: the world's hardship and your personal abundance can coexist, because one doesn't erase or invalidate the other. In fact, allowing yourself to fully receive and celebrate your blessings is what gives you the strength and compassion to pour back into others from overflow, not depletion.

Client Story: From Blocked to Abundant in Love and Money

One of my clients, whom I'll call, Melanie, came to me after years of dealing with her toxic ex-partner and had a financial life that also mirrored this. As we worked together, it became clear that Melanie had deeply embedded scarcity beliefs.

She believed she had to overwork and prove her worth when it came to her relationships as well as her job. In fact, when we worked together, she was healing from one toxic relationship whilst trying to dodge another one. If this wasn't enough, she was simultaneously struggling to keep up with bills and maintain a roof over her head.

Through private coaching, Melanie began to shift her mindset and energy. She practiced forgiveness of her past patterns which was a huge part of her healing. She soon realized that nothing changed in her present reality because she continued to reinforce the strength of her belief. This core belief made her feel that there was something intrinsically wrong with her no matter what she chose to do in life, and she did not deserve any more than she already had.

From our time together, she learned how to receive without feeling automatically guilty, or that she had to reciprocate by giving back to the person immediately afterwards to "settle the score." She learned how to stop settling for low-paid jobs that were not a true reflection of her worth or expertise, and she finally stopped over-functioning in relationships. She integrated a number of coaching tools I shared with her, alongside practical strategies to reset her relationship with money.

Within months, she not only met a partner who treated her with respect and consistency, but she also launched the business she had been thinking about for years.

For the first time, she had a financial strategy that allowed her to finally start putting money towards her savings from a place of overflow. As you can see, Melanie didn't "choose" between love and wealth because she aligned herself to receive both. **Even when it looked like she wasn't going to make it.**

CHAPTER 15

LIVING YOUR HIGHEST LOVE TIMELINE

By now, you've done the inner work, reset your standards, started looking at the different layers of your core wounds, and started thinking about how to implement something new to start attracting higher caliber connections. But the real transformation happens when you fully embody the woman who not only attracts but effortlessly sustains her worthiest, most aligned relationships.

It is now time that we talk about you stepping into your **highest love timeline:** This is your new reality where you trust yourself, your desires, and the higher powers above to deliver the partnership you deserve. This is the chapter where you realize: You were never "too much," "too ambitious," or "too late." Love has always been available to you. You just needed to become just as available to it, so it could find you.

WHAT IS YOUR HIGHEST LOVE TIMELINE?

Your highest love timeline is the reality where:

- You no longer settle for anything less than deep, mutual, soul-expanding love.

- You embody the woman who is magnetic and worthy of it all.

- You balance love and ambition effortlessly.

- You attract partners who meet you on every level.

This timeline is not a fantasy. It is a choice you make every single day: in the way you show up and in the standards you hold from now on.

SUSTAINING YOUR HIGHEST TIMELINE

One thing is living according to your highest timeline, and another thing is sustaining it. Life is going to bring you relationships that will test your new standards and boundaries. And I won't lie, sometimes you will fall off and forget some of the things you learned along the way. That's perfectly fine!

Don't forget that you are a human being, and it is bound to happen. Unfortunately, you can't always see what's coming. But what you can do is stay in the energy of the student at all times and just take things that do not work out as lessons to better equip you for the next opportunity.

Living your highest love timeline isn't about perfection. It's about continuing to prioritize your self-worth; choosing alignment over harmful attachments; staying open and receptive without abandoning yourself and above all, leading with trust and clarity, not fear.

You will get the exact soulmate partnership that you desire. It is inevitable. What is required of you is not beauty; it is not a bunch of psychology certificates or even any woo-woo rituals! It requires daily embodiment of what you want in all areas of your life; in other words:

- How you speak to yourself.

- How you date.

- How you communicate your needs.

- How you maintain your boundaries.

What you need to keep in mind also, is that this work is not something you complete overnight. It is an ongoing practice that will require you to always be ready to learn something new when it comes to your own personal path. Learning to surrender and knowing that you will always come out the other side better off, however, is half the challenge in being successful in love. Before we close, I want to remind you of the free trainings available to support your journey:

The Science of Attraction: How High-Achieving Women Can Rewire for Real Emotional Intimacy

In this training, I help you understand the psychology and energetics of attraction so you can create deep emotional connection without dimming your ambition or authenticity.

You'll discover:

1. Why your success-driven wiring can sometimes interfere with emotional connection.

2. How to realign your success without sacrificing your ambition.

3. How attraction isn't just chemistry, it's energy and perception.

4. How high-achieving women can unintentionally project self-sufficiency in ways that block deeper intimacy.

Healing the Three Love Wounds: How to End Emotionally Unavailable Cycles for Good

In this training, we'll move beyond awareness of the three core love wounds into *embodiment and transformation*, helping you shift the patterns that have been keeping you stuck in love.

You'll discover:

1. A deeper understanding of each core wound: how they form, how they show up in your emotional

landscape, and how to begin softening its hold on your relationships.

2. The link between your nervous system, attachment style, and emotional responses, so you can move from reaction to regulation.

3. A practical tool to begin rewiring old patterns and open yourself to love that feels deeply fulfilling.

Becoming the Woman Who Attracts Her Equal

In this training, I show you how to embody the energy, mindset, and boundaries of a woman who naturally attracts and sustains a high-quality, emotionally available partnership.

You'll discover:

1. How to shift from chasing or over-performing in love to *receiving* and allowing partnership to meet you with ease.

2. The energetic and behavioral traits of women who naturally attract emotionally available men and keep them.

3. How to show up as your authentic, high-value self in dating and relationships without playing games or compromising your standards.

HOW TO ACCESS YOUR BONUS TRAININGS

1. **Go to** https://www.rachelroseonline.com/ .

2. Select "Video Trainings."
3. Select the relevant training for this chapter and use code "YOUAREWORTHY" at checkout for free access.

These trainings are not just content; they are activations. Revisit them whenever you need a reminder of your power. Yes, this book is about dating your worth, but if you haven't realized it yet, the most important relationship first and foremost is with yourself. From there, your romantic relationships are a reflection and external manifestation of how deep you are willing to go with your own spirit.

PERSONAL STORY: MY HIGHEST TIMELINE UNLOCKED

I want to end this book by sharing a very real and personal story. There was a time when I believed love wasn't for me. Yes, I was the "successful one" in every room but I felt isolated and unseen in my romantic life. I was always the butt of everyone's joke as the one with the constant tragic stories, and I watched as all my friends were able to have relationships with so much ease.

When I finally did the deep inner work I've shared in this book, when I started healing my core wounds and accepting them for what they are, when I redefined love, when I trusted myself and stopped over-functioning...everything shifted. I was finally capable of holding serious relationships that were *real.* Men started to see me fully, love me more deeply, and match me energetically. I had to rewrite my own blueprint as to what love really meant for me, even when I had no template at all to learn from. I always thought I was a bit unfortunate in that sense, but now I realize that it is the biggest gift of all.

But the best part? I realized relationships aren't the prize. **The woman I became in the process was.**

About 11 years ago or so, just before I really embarked on my own profound spiritual journey, I was working in an educational setting and one of my colleagues was a child psychologist. She asked me randomly one day in one of our deep chats about which relationships I had the fondest memories of. I remember I stayed quiet as I tried to rack my brain. I couldn't give her *one single example* of a healthy relationship because, for me, love just meant you battled through it. For me, love meant that you separated, and then came back to the vicious cycle of more games and emotional abuse. That is literally all I knew at that point.

If you ask me now? I am so grateful to say that I have been blessed with some of the most passionate men in my lifetime to date. That yes, of course, every relationship has its ups and downs but I could die tomorrow and say that I loved each of these men so deeply, and they each gave me a gift of their own that was irreplaceable and quintessential to my growth.

I changed love into a spiritual and alchemical process. The longest relationship of my life felt like I was with the best friend I never had, and to this day, I swear that he healed so many parts of me, even the parts I thought were chronically broken. He is part of the reason why my capacity to love is so expansive today.

The past two years have been the epitome of transformation and rebirth. I faced a sudden health crisis that nearly cost me my life, and not long after, the man I had fallen in love with in my twenties — who had recently come back into my life — shared that he was battling a chronic illness and wanted to spend the rest of his life alone, instead of building one together.

Through it all, I was supported by an incredible network of people who carried me through the hardest moments, allowing me to continue guiding women around the world as they redefined love on every level for themselves.

And now? If I'm being completely honest, I thought this book would end differently. But if there's one thing you've learned about me by now, it's that I live and love with radical honesty.

Lately, there's a lightness in my days and a calm kind of excitement that feels like love is finding its way back in. After all the shadow work, I no longer need certainty to feel at peace. There's beauty in letting life unfold, in trusting that what's meant for me will arrive in its own time, in its own way.

It has taken thirty-six years of learning, unlearning, and choosing myself over and over to arrive here: **grounded and quietly open to what's ahead.** And maybe that's exactly how this book was always meant to end...not perfectly, but truthfully.

I'm not at the "happily ever after" part just yet, but I'm absolutely on the right page. My love life has become a reflection of everything you've read: soft, empowered, joyful, and aligned.

Something beautiful is unfolding... and I have a feeling the next chapter will be worth writing about, too.

PART FOUR: JOURNAL REFLECTION AND AFFIRMATIONS

Expansion is the natural by-product of alignment. When you're no longer operating from fear, life meets you where you are — in overflow.

This part is about receiving **more**: more love, more wealth, more joy. You are safe to expand because you now have the inner foundation to sustain it.

PROMPTS:

1. **Redefining "Having It All"**
   Your definition of success evolves as you do.
   What does "having it all" truly mean for me now when it comes to love and wealth?

2. **Capacity to Receive**
   Receiving requires nervous system safety, not luck.
   Where do I still resist abundance, and how can I expand my capacity to receive it with ease?

3. **Next-Level Identity**
   Imagine your next chapter as if it's already happening.
   Who is the next-level version of me in love and life, and how can I start showing up as her today?

4. **Celebration as Magnetism**
   Gratitude and celebration create momentum.
   How can I celebrate how far I've come, even before reaching my next goal?

5. **Living Your Highest Timeline**
   The universe mirrors what you believe you deserve.
   What would my highest love timeline feel like if I allowed it to fully unfold now?

CONCLUSION: YOU ARE WORTHY OF IT ALL

Congratulations, you made it to the end of this book, but in truth, this is just the beginning.

By now, you have learned that love is not a reward for perfection or for sacrifice. It is not reserved only for those who fit a mold or follow outdated rules. It is available to you because you exist, because you are worthy, and because now that you are in this part of your life's journey, you are ready to receive it.

You have seen how everything that society tells you is "too much" about you actually makes you magnetic, and a premium candidate for attracting the right partner when you know how to channel your gifts in a way that serves your highest good.

This book was not solely about teaching you how to find love. It was about helping you remember that despite where you live on the planet or what experiences you have had to date, love has always been within your reach the entire time.

I hope you close this book recognizing that you can have everything you have always dreamed of and you will...**once you make the decision that it is your birthright to receive it.**

You are worthy of it all.

YOUR JOURNEY CONTINUES

The guidance and stories I've shared in this book are just the start. Real transformation happens when you integrate these lessons into your dating approach and your relationship with yourself.

Within my signature program, **Attract Your Equal**, we'll take everything you've learned here and turn it into embodied action, so you're no longer just understanding love differently, you're *living* it.

If this book resonated with you, this is your next chapter: an intimate, five-month journey to attract a partner who meets you at your level, on every level. Use the link below to find out more about what the program involves and whether this is a fit for you:

HOW TO FIND OUT MORE ABOUT THE 'ATTRACT YOUR EQUAL' PROGRAM

1. **Go to** https://www.rachelroseonline.com/ .

2. **Select** "Work With Me."

3. **Select** "Attract Your Equal."

FINAL AFFIRMATION

Repeat this to yourself as often as you need:

I am worthy of love, success, and abundance. I am safe to receive everything I desire. I attract relationships that reflect my highest self. I choose partnership without sacrifice. I am living my highest love timeline.

You were never meant to settle. You were always meant to rise.

And now, you have everything you need to claim it all.

THE LOVE AND ALIGNMENT TOOLKIT

By the time you've reached this part of the book, something in you has already shifted.

You've looked at yourself honestly and you've begun the inner rewiring that so many women avoid, because it's easier to point outward than to turn inward.

That alone is something to celebrate.

Most people stop at awareness. They read the books, nod along to the lessons, and understand what needs to change but they never actually *live* it.

But you're not most people and this is where your awareness transforms into embodiment. Awareness happens in your mind. Embodiment happens in your body, your habits, your energy, and your day-to-day decisions. It's when everything you've learned begins to *show up through you,* not as something you're forcing, but as something you've become.

The truth is that the woman who attracts her equal doesn't try to be magnetic...she simply *is*. Her magnetism is the natural by-product of living in integrity with her worth. She doesn't chase validation; *she radiates self-trust*. She doesn't perform for love; *she anchors in love.*

The five tools in this chapter are here to keep you grounded in that embodiment. Think of them as your "energetic anchors," or as your practices that bring you back home when you drift into fear. They'll help you regulate your emotions, reconnect with your feminine energy, and stay in alignment with the love and life you're calling in.

1. THE SELF-WORTH CALIBRATION TOOL

No matter how self-aware or emotionally intelligent you become, there will always be moments where your energy wobbles. You might find yourself re-reading a text message over and over, wondering what he meant. You might catch yourself trying to prove your value by giving too much or bending your boundaries in the hope that someone will recognize your effort. And in those moments, you might forget just how magnetic you already are.

That's when it's time to recalibrate.

This tool is simple but life-changing when practiced consistently. When you notice yourself slipping into "prove mode," pause. Literally stop what you're doing. Drop your shoulders. Inhale deeply. Feel your feet on the ground. Let your body remind you that you are safe, supported, and whole.

Then, speak this truth out loud:

"I am already full. This situation is a bonus."

This is more than a mantra, because as you can see, it's an energetic correction. It shifts you from scarcity to abundance, from proving to embodying. This way, you're no longer approaching love or life from emptiness, but you're instead sharing from fullness.

You stop asking, *"What do I need to do to keep this?"*
And start remembering, *"Nothing that's meant for me requires performance."*

When you hold this energy, people feel it. You become the woman who knows her worth so deeply that she doesn't chase or force anything. She allows, and in allowing... she becomes irresistible.

Use this recalibration whenever you feel off-balance, for example, after a triggering conversation or a moment where you start to doubt yourself. With time you will see that self-worth isn't a feeling you "find," but it's a frequency you return to—over and over again.

2. NERVOUS SYSTEM RESET

You cannot attract secure love from an unsafe body. When you're triggered, i.e. when someone pulls away, sends a confusing message, or doesn't show up how you expected—your nervous system often interprets that as danger. Suddenly, your body floods with cortisol and adrenaline, and your brain goes into panic mode. That's when you do the things you later regret: over-text, over-explain, or in the extreme cases, reactively block and delete this person from your life.

This isn't weakness. It's biology. Your body is trying to find safety in the only way it knows how...through control. The problem though is that love can't grow in control. Love grows in calm. So before you act, you have to learn to self-regulate in order to really give love a fair chance at thriving.

Here's a reset ritual you can do anytime, anywhere:

1. **Inhale through your nose for four counts.**
   Feel your chest and belly rise.

2. **Exhale slowly through your mouth for six counts.**
   Imagine tension leaving your body with each breath.

3. **Drop your shoulders. Unclench your jaw.**
   Soften your stomach and let yourself expand.

4. **Place one hand on your heart and say aloud:**
   "I am safe in love. I am safe in this moment."

Repeat this until your body feels soft again.

This isn't just breathing, it's communicating safety to your nervous system. You're teaching your body that discomfort is not danger and that uncertainty is not abandonment. Do this before you respond to a triggering message, before you spiral into overthinking someone's intentions, or even before a first date. With practice, this will be the calm that allows genuine intimacy to unfold.

3. ENERGY AUDIT

Every time you over-give or engage with something that drains you, you leak energy. As a result, when your energy is scattered, you start attracting people and experiences that match that frequency.

Your energy is your most sacred currency because it's how the Universe and everyone around you read your vibration. This is why protecting it isn't optional; it's essential.

The Energy Audit is your weekly ritual for realignment. It's how you stay connected to what nourishes you and release what doesn't. At the end of each week, take ten quiet minutes and ask yourself:

- What fueled me this week? (What made me feel alive, peaceful, or grounded?)

- What drained me? (What left me feeling anxious, small, or off-center?)

- What felt forced? (What did I do out of obligation instead of alignment?)

Be radically honest. Sometimes, the things draining you aren't obvious. They might be that one friendship that always revolves around venting, the social media scroll that leaves you comparing yourself to strangers, or the man you keep "giving another chance" to even though your gut already knows he is no good for you.

Once you identify your leaks, decide how to shift your energy for the following week. That might mean setting a boundary or simply stepping back. Remember: every time you say no to what drains you, you create space for what aligns with you. When your energy is clean and aligned, love starts finding you effortlessly—because your field is finally clear enough to receive it.

4. FEMININE ENERGY RECONNECTION

High-achieving women tend to spend most of their time in masculine energy because it's how we've survived, and it's how we've succeeded. As we have discussed earlier in the book, the energy that builds your career isn't the same energy that builds connection.

Feminine energy on the other hand is receptive, intuitive, creative, and magnetic. It's what allows you to *feel* deeply instead of analyzing everything. It's what helps you trust instead of chase. When you find yourself over-functioning: texting first all the time, trying to plan every step of the connection, or feeling tense and "on guard"—it's time to come home to your feminine flow.

Try this:

1. **Move your body.** Put on music that makes you feel beautiful—something sensual or grounding. Close your eyes and move however your body wants to. Don't perform, don't try and be perfect—just *feel*. This releases tension and reconnects you to your natural rhythm.

2. **Touch your body with presence.** Place one hand on your heart, the other on your lower belly. Breathe slowly and imagine light filling you from the inside out. This small act of self-touch teaches your body that softness is safe again.

3. **Speak to yourself gently.** Instead of "Why am I like this?", try "It's okay. I'm learning to trust myself."

This is the art of feminine embodiment: learning to listen to your inner cues instead of overriding them. Your feminine energy is not something you have to perform or pretend to have. It's who you already are underneath the armor. When you're anchored in that softness, men who thrive on control, confusion, and power games can no longer reach you. You're operating from a completely different vibration, the kind that commands genuine devotion, not just surface-level attention.

5. MANIFESTATION INTEGRATION

Manifestation is not about sitting on your couch wishing for love to magically appear. It's also not about pretending you're happy when you're not. Real manifestation is about alignment. It's when your thoughts, emotions, and actions are telling the same story. Most people say they want love but they think thoughts of fear, feel emotions of doubt, and take actions from scarcity. They affirm, "I'm ready for love," while still entertaining situations that make them feel unsafe or unseen. They visualize a healthy relationship but still text the emotionally unavailable ex.

Manifestation begins when you start *living like the woman who already has what she desires.* Here's how to integrate it:

Each morning, take two minutes to visualize the relationship you want. Not the *fantasy,* but the *feeling.*

Ask yourself:

What does peace feel like in my body?
What does being emotionally supported feel like in my chest?
What does safety feel like in my nervous system?

Let those sensations flood your body. Then, carry that energy into your day.

Before you make a decision, ask:

Does this action reflect the woman who already has what she wants?
Would she text back out of anxiety?
Would she settle for inconsistency?
Would she abandon herself to feel chosen?
Or would she take a breath, smile, and trust that what's meant for her is already aligning behind the scenes?

That's manifestation in motion.

Every time you choose faith over fear, you're signaling to the higher powers above that you're ready and this is when life starts rearranging itself in your favor.

CLOSING NOTE

These five tools aren't meant to make you "perfect." They're meant to help you stay anchored. There will still be days where you slip up and that's okay. You're human. The point isn't to never fall, it's to come home faster each time. These practices are how you do that. They're your roadmap back to peace when you lose your footing.

The more you practice these tools, the more natural they become. You'll stop needing constant reminders because you'll start *embodying* the energy you once had to consciously create.

And that's when the magic happens.

You'll notice the people, opportunities, and love you once chased start showing up with ease. You'll look around and realize that you didn't have to fight for anything. You simply had to become the version of yourself who already had it.

That's embodiment. That's alignment.

And that's what it truly means to **date your worth.**

RECOMMENDED READING

These are the books I most often recommend to clients and women on the same journey of self-worth, emotional healing, and aligned love. Each one explores a different dimension of what it means to lead from wholeness. As with everything I have mentioned in this book, take what resonates, leave what doesn't, and let the rest meet you when you're ready.

LOVE, ATTACHMENT & BOUNDARIES

Attached — *Dr. Amir Levine & Rachel S. F. Heller, M.A.*

Why Him? Why Her? — *Helen Fisher*

Set Boundaries, Find Peace — *Nedra Glover Tawwab*

THE ENERGY OF SURRENDER & SELF MASTERY

Let Them Theory — *Mel Robbins & Sawyer Robbins*

Radical Acceptance — *Tara Brach*

Power vs. Force — *David R. Hawkins, M.D., Ph.D.*

MANIFESTATION, HEALING & ABUNDANCE

Rich as F*ck — *Amanda Frances*

Ask and It Is Given — *Esther & Jerry Hicks*

You Can Heal Your Life — *Louise Hay*

EPILOGUE: THE EVOLUTION OF YOU

There will come a moment when you'll realize that you are no longer the same woman who first picked up this book. Something subtle but irreversible has shifted. You've grown quieter inside, but stronger. You've questioned patterns that once ruled your life, and softened into parts of yourself that once felt unsafe to touch. You've begun to hear your own voice again, and more importantly, to trust it.

That is what evolution feels like. It doesn't happen in the way the world tells you it should. For example, there's no cinematic background music or spotlight moment when everything suddenly makes sense. It happens slowly, in those quiet, sacred moments when you choose differently.

The woman you are today has earned her softness. Through heartbreaks, self-doubt and a relentless pursuit of "more," she has discovered that true power lies in being at peace with herself. This is the kind of peace that doesn't need validation or applause.

The world will always try to convince you that you need to be more to deserve love: prettier, thinner, calmer, wealthier, more confident, etc. It's a lifelong illusion that keeps so many women chasing something that was never missing in the first place. **But not you.** *You are remembering that your worth was never up for negotiation.*

If this book has done its job, it's reminded you that the most magnetic version of you isn't the woman who's mastered the game — it's the woman who no longer needs to play it. This is the version of you who doesn't perform, but simply *is*.

You've probably noticed that the women who appear to live with ease and attract love, money, etc., all have one thing in common: they've stopped performing for approval. They recognize that the right opportunities come from alignment, not overexertion. And that's the space you are stepping into now.

It's not that the lessons end here; they just evolve. The same woman who used to chase closure will now choose clarity. And the same woman who once begged for crumbs will now expect a seat at the table — *or build her own.* You've met different versions of yourself in these pages, and maybe, for the first time, you've allowed them all to coexist without shame. You've begun to see that you can be both ambitious and soft, both independent and deeply connected, and both the woman who builds empires and the woman who allows herself to be held.

It takes a special kind of courage to love after you've been hurt but it takes even more courage to do it consciously, with awareness. Because once you know better, there is no going back to how you used to operate. You start seeing everything through a new lens and that awareness changes you at your core. It doesn't mean you'll never be triggered again or that you won't attract challenges. It means you'll meet them differently.

You'll notice when your nervous system starts to spiral and know exactly what it's asking for. You'll stop overexplaining your worth to people who can't see it. You'll feel the difference between anxiety and intuition. From that place, love no longer becomes something you chase because it becomes something you allow into your life with ease, and receive with grace. When you are anchored in your worth, you stop seeking validation. You become magnetic to the very things that once eluded you — kindness, consistency, commitment and safety.

The woman who attracts from her healed energy isn't desperate for attention. **She doesn't demand to be chosen because she's already chosen herself.** When you learn to meet yourself with compassion, life meets you with abundance. That's why I always say: the way you love yourself is the way you'll allow the world to love you.

You'll start to notice it in small, beautiful ways that this has become your new reality:

A calm in your chest when someone doesn't text back.
A smile when you look in the mirror instead of scanning for flaws.
A deep exhale when you realize you no longer want to chase people, because you trust that what's meant for you cannot miss you.

Wherever you are on your journey right now, you are exactly where you're supposed to be. If love hasn't arrived yet, it's not because you're behind. It's because your story is still being written. And when it does arrive, when the person who can meet you at the depth of your truth appears, you'll recognize them instantly, because their energy will feel like peace.

Until then, keep becoming *her:* the woman who attracts from wholeness. Keep building your life and your peace. Let your heart stay open, but your standards stay strong. Be the woman who chooses herself, every single day. If you ever doubt that you're making progress, remember this: every boundary and every brave decision to walk away from what no longer fits is you rewriting your love story in real time.

And maybe that's the real message of this book: **you don't need to become someone else to attract the life and love you want. You just need to remember who you are.**

ACKNOWLEDGEMENTS

TO MY FAMILY

To my family — thank you for putting up with every wild idea I've ever had and loving me through all of them anyway. Thank you for supporting me through relationships that were sometimes beautiful, sometimes brutal, and always meaningful in shaping the woman and coach I am today. Every experience has brought me closer to my purpose, and I carry the strength of where I come from in every word of this book.

TO MY FRIENDS

Thank you to my friends (my chosen family) for always believing in me, holding me accountable to my purpose, and never letting me forget who I am, even when I momentarily did. Thank you for cheering through every creative burst and breakdown, for your laughter, your patience, and your unwavering belief that I was meant to do something extraordinary. You've each held space for me in your own way, and this book exists because of that love.

TO MY CREATIVE TEAM

To my incredible designer — thank you for your patience, grace, and devotion during this process. You've created magic again, all while embracing new chapters in your own life — a marriage and a beautiful baby. And to my editor, thank you for your calm strength, compassion, and brilliance in tightening this vision even through your own life transitions. You both worked tirelessly and cut your timelines in half to make this release possible — I see you, and I'm so grateful for you.

TO THE DIVINE TIMING OF IT ALL

To God, the Universe, and my angels — thank you for granting me another season in life when it wasn't clear I would have one. Thank you for every miracle and redirection that brought me here. I am humbled to be walking into this next chapter of my life and work renewed, grateful, and ready.

And to the person who reminded me what it feels like to be truly seen — thank you. No matter what the future holds, I'll always honor the way your presence reawakened my capacity for love.

Rachel Rose, originally from London, is a certified Relationship and Boundaries Coach known for her intuitive, evidence-based, and results-driven approach to modern love. Since 2020, she has been guiding ambitious, self-aware women to redefine how they approach dating and relationships, all while maintaining their power.

With a background in neuroscience, psychology, and energy healing, Rachel empowers conscious and accomplished women to date with clarity and unwavering self-worth. She has been **featured in New York City's Times Square** as well as **major international publications including** *Cosmopolitan* **and** *Glamour*, where her insights on feminine energy, emotional intelligence, and relationship dynamics have resonated with women around the world.

Rachel credits her success to her unique ability to merge both science and soul, combining the rigor of psychology and neuroscience with intuitive emotional understanding. She has helped transform the lives of women across **four continents to date**, showing them what's possible not only in love but in every area of life. And she doesn't plan to stop there.

Currently completing her **master's degree in Psychology and Neuroscience of Mental Health at King's College London,** Rachel hopes to pursue a **PhD** in the near future to further deepen her understanding of human behavior and how the brain shapes our experience of love and self-worth.

Her renowned signature program, **Attract Your Equal**, has become a life-changing experience for women worldwide: a framework that helps them break free from patterns of self-sabotage, elevate their standards, and call in emotionally available, high-quality partners who are ready to meet them at their level. The transformations her clients experience extend well beyond romantic relationships, influencing their careers, family dynamics, health, wellbeing, and sense of overall life alignment.

Rachel also offers shorter, intimate **private coaching containers**, where she works one-on-one with women seeking targeted transformation in specific areas of love, boundaries, and personal power. Her clients often say her work bridges the head and the heart, bringing both deep self-awareness and practical guidance for real-world change.

www.ingramcontent.com/pod-product-compliance
Lightning Source LLC
Chambersburg PA
CBHW030321080526
44584CB00012B/657